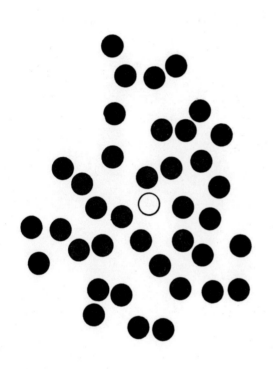

# SCARCITY
# AND EVIL

# SCARCITY AND EVIL

*by Vivian Charles Walsh*

PRENTICE-HALL, INC.
*Englewood Cliffs, N.J.,* 1961

Printed in the United States of America
79154-C

# Acknowledgments

An early version of part of Chapter One appeared in *Philosophy of Science,* under the title "Scarcity and the Concepts of Ethics," and part of Chapter Two in the *Journal of Philosophy,* under the title "Ascriptions and Appraisals." Part of Chapter Three was published in the *Cambridge Journal,* as "The Theory of the Good Will." I am indebted to the Editors of these Journals for their permission to use this material here.

Throughout the development of these ideas I have been helped by the advice of numerous friends. Professor G. A. Duncan of Dublin University gave me my first encouragement; Professor Ernest Nagel of Columbia University made valuable suggestions; Professor Hilary Putnam of Princeton University read every version of this work, and his help was invaluable. The faults that remain are quite characteristically my own.

The characters and incidents which illustrate the argument of this work were constructed solely with that purpose in mind, and bear no intentional relation to any real persons or happenings.

V.C.W.

# Contents

Introduction, 1

Chapter One, 11

Chapter Two, 45

Chapter Three, 67

Chapter Four, 85

Conclusion, 103

# SCARCITY
# AND EVIL

# Introduction

In speaking of most people, and most of the time, we are prepared to make use of settled idioms, even when these do not exactly fit. Habit, laziness and sheer lack of time compel this. But just now and then our preoccupation with somebody grows so great that we find ourselves realizing how ill fitted to describe them are all the phrases at our disposal. At times such as these, we come to notice, through interest in its application to a particular case, what is in fact some general peculiarity or inconsistency of language. When we are most keenly aware of the near presence of un-discovered and intensely interesting human qualities, we notice the blurred picture which our efforts at description give us back.

It is not that the questions discussed at length in this book arise only, or even most strictly, when speaking of the situation of the one or two people whose predicament first suggested them to me: these problems once noticed are seen to arise in any effort to give an account of a certain aspect of human experience; it is merely that their significance was first borne upon me in particular cases. Nothing more will be said here about the origin of the ideas which I now propose to put forward; it is mentioned only in the hope that it would throw light on the way in which logical problems (at their face value not particularly personal or intimate) sometimes are suggested, and how their solutions may be in turn applied.

A group of puzzles, known to ancient writers simply as "the problem of evil," is rarely discussed today by philosophers. Thoughtful people who are not professional philosophers—novelists, poets, artists of all kinds—find themselves wanting to raise questions which would once have been described as being about the nature of evil. Such people are disappointed to find that philosophers today are silent on these matters. Yet the silence can be explained and in part justified; it is probable that some of the questions which it used to be supposed to be possible to ask about evil were not in fact genuine questions at all, so that it is not to the point to attempt to answer them.

In one sense, what used to be called "the problem of evil" is not a philosophical problem—strictly speaking, it is not a "problem" at all. If it is true that philosophical problems are about our concepts, then such problems can be shown to arise in the attempt to construe some of the concepts involved in ordinary discussions of evil. But this is not what is normally meant by speaking of "the problem of evil." This phrase is often used to indicate not an unsettled theoretical question to which an answer is conceivable, but a brute fact which confronts us with a "problem" in the sense of a stumbling block, of a surd quality in our experi-

ence which we cannot get around and which may re-
duce us to despair.

Of course, philosophy cannot in principle provide
an answer to "the problem of evil" in this sense. We
of this generation cannot, like Boethius, derive such
consolations from philosophy. But this is not to say
that philosophical analysis has nothing to offer us in
dealing with these matters; it is one thing to be able
and willing to face facts, and quite another thing to
know exactly what it is appropriate to say about them.
We cannot solve the "problem of evil" by philosophy
in the old heroic sense of removing, by a dialectical
sleight of hand, the evil of the world. But we can show
more clearly than is always obvious what exactly is
implied by the statements we make about evil, and
the principal concepts in terms of which we order our
observations on the matter.

What used to be lumped together under the title,
"the problem of evil," is a tangle of puzzles of many
different sorts. It does not follow that because some
are pseudo-problems all are. Many of the classic writings on this topic are capable of two significantly different interpretations: they can be taken as making
heroic but absurd claims, and dismissed as nonsense;
or they can be taken as over-dramatized statements
of more limited claims about the nature of concepts connected with evil. Unless we are more concerned with debunking traditional philosophy than
with discovering the truth, the latter interpretation
is perhaps the more fruitful. Taken thus, some of the
questions raised by ancient writers on evil can be

shown to be significant, and can be restated in ways which make it clear that they do not depend for their force upon preoccupation with illusory issues.

This book is a modern discussion of such questions. It is written as philosophy and for philosophers, but I believe that it may also interest those who turn to philosophy in the hope that it will clarify issues which have arisen in their personal experience. There has been much talk since the thirties about philosophy being "contentless," being merely "analysis" and just "verbal." Philosophy is, of course, "contentless" in the sense that it is concerned with the analysis of the logical behavior of concepts, as such. It is "verbal" in the sense that, in order to investigate concepts expressed in ordinary words, one must examine the ways in which these words behave. But the "verbal" mistakes which philosophers try to correct are mistakes about concepts and the consequences of such mistakes are very far indeed from being merely linguistic. Even if doing philosophy can still not return to being a matter of enunciating "philosophical propositions" about the traditional "great questions," it does not follow that philosophical analysis cannot be applied to some of the questions which ordinary people feel it ought to discuss. If we are to be sincere in our respect for ordinary usage we must recognize that questions about the nature of evil would be understood by ordinary people, who would have at least a pretty good notion about what was being asked.

Outside of philosophy proper I have found one notion which has been extremely helpful, namely, the

economic concept of "scarcity." The introduction of a
term from technical economics may seem strange in
this context, for many people who are not immediately
concerned with modern work on economic scope and
method still, reasonably enough, regard economic matters simply as those concerned with getting our bread
and butter and economic science as a technical spe-
cialty offering no concepts of interest to the philosopher. But the economic relation of "scarcity" has a
much wider application than is usually realized by non-
economists, for it holds between any means which we
may require and any end at which we may be aiming
when the means are not sufficient for the complete attainment of that end. The means required to achieve
any of the ends of action—for example, of moral action
—may differ greatly among themselves; but they may
all be scarce, in the sense that they have to be econ-
omized—there "may not be enough to go around."

The concept of scarcity is admittedly a highly ab-
stract one. Nevertheless, it is precisely for this reason
that it has special advantages, and even at this stage we
may notice one or two of the more obvious points in its
favor. In Kant's system, for example, the equivalent
of this notion of scarcity consists of the admission that a
good will may lack certain things which are needed
for the attainment of the will's objects. By concen-
trating on particular scarce things, Kant fails to do
justice to the range of the effects of scarcity.

It will become apparent in the course of this work
that one obtains a more general treatment when one
considers scarcity explicitly, rather than just this, that,

or the other scarce thing. Secondly, concentration on the relation of scarcity to other concepts frees us from distractions introduced into other treatments by the consideration at the same time of certain vivid non-economic characteristics of some of the things which are scarce.

The word "pain," for instance, may suggest very well the intensity with which a certain type of experience is *felt,* but it does not draw attention to what is peculiarly economic in the situation. Some even quite trivial instances of scarcity may cause "pain" or be noticed as "crying evils," and the urgency of these cases may draw attention to the particular loss involved; but an analysis conducted in terms of such notions cannot take us to the core of the matter, from which pain is given off as a spark from the clash of irreconcilables.

In the chapters that follow, I shall first of all have to satisfy the reader that what I have chosen to call "the economic aspect of experience" is pointedly so described; I shall show how situations which seem to have little or nothing in common all contain instances of what I have called scarcity. I believe that few people at the moment—whether philosophers or not—realize that there is an important similarity between obvious, well-known instances of the scarcity of economic goods, and moral choice and the hindrances to which it is subject.

After establishing that our experience has an economic aspect in the sense which I intend, and that the word "scarcity" is appropriately used as I am using it, it will then be my concern to explore the implications of this for philosophy. I shall first of all try to show that if the implications of what I call "scarcity" are once understood, then a number of philosophical notions need reconsidering—including some of the most widely accepted of contemporary views about moral responsibility.

Perhaps we may anticipate one or two of what seem to be the more interesting points which arise in the course of the discussion. As it turns out, there is an intimate connection between the economic relation of scarcity and the type of subject matter about which most ethical statements are made. It has been customary for some time to distinguish between ethical words and certain other words with different, though related, functions. Once the nature and significance of the economic relation is clearly seen, it becomes apparent that it is vital to distinguish between usages which are appropriate when speaking about this relation and those which are appropriate in ethical statements properly so called.

Consider, for instance, the behavior of the words we ordinarily use in speaking about certain everyday situations. On being told of some piece of behavior which is judged to be wrong, it would be perfectly idiomatic English to comment, "How very immoral!" or, "What a shocking piece of immorality!" It would be equally natural to make remarks like, "He has failed to do his duty," "He ought not to have acted in this way," and so on.

Now suppose we learn more about the situation: a

doctor has failed to give his patient the necessary treatment, but—we are now told—this was only because they were at sea together in a small yacht without medical supplies, or because at the time of this case the required treatment was only being developed and could not yet be known to the doctor. In the light of this new information the sort of comment quoted above would no longer pertain; instead, we should hear, "What a tragic thing to happen," or, "What a terrible pity." Now the new information was in fact a statement of the economic type: the doctor was prevented from curing his patient by the scarcity of certain required means.

The distinction which ordinary ethical words observe when they behave in the way indicated above has always been of great interest to philosophers, who have attempted to express it by means of a number of familiar technical notations. Philosophers presumably have wanted these technical notations because, although ordinary ethical words indicate the distinction in much of their behavior, they do not always adhere to it consistently. Deontologists, for instance, made technical distinctions between "objective rightness," "subjective rightness," "objective duty," and "subjective duty." In ordinary language one can speak only of right or wrong actions; in ordinary language the doctor would have to be said to have failed to do the right thing—though of course it would be added that this was not his fault; he had done the best he could under the circumstances.

In the chapter that follows we shall consider separately some of the different elements which can be distinguished in such sentences. We shall begin by investigating what we are doing when we describe someone as subject to "strains," suffering from "hindrances," or from the "scarcity" or "lack" of some requisite. This first chapter is in effect an examination of the behavior of economic words and can be regarded as a philosophical analysis of the subject matter of economics.

# I.

**M**ost economists would agree today that there is a distinguishably economic aspect of experience. Earlier writers, led by a desire to keep their scientific discussions within certain limits, tried indeed to work on the assumption that there was a certain economic *part* of experience—that we could select a particular part of our experience, put a fence around it and call it "economic experience." All the numerous efforts to indicate where this fence should be situated have, however, failed, and after much bitter controversy, the tendency now is to say that such attempts were foredoomed, because they misunderstood the nature of the economic problem. They treated what could in fact be one aspect of *any* of our experiences as if it was the whole of some experience.

The only objection which is still urged against the "aspect" view by writers conversant with the literature of the recent past is one which only concerns the practice of a technical economist; it is sometimes still urged that the class of people called professional economists cannot be expected to subject to detailed analysis the economic aspect of every sort of experience. It is indeed a convenient practical expedient to have people who make it their job to analyze exclusively the economic aspect of a certain part of our daily lives—people who write about the economic aspect of full employment, the economic aspect of population, and the like. These are the only sort of matter which the man in the street yet regards as "economic." But this is a case where, as Berkeley would have put it, one should think with the learned and speak with the vulgar.

In any case the view which we have been discussing does not claim to be a theoretical refutation of the claim that all experience may have an economic aspect; it is merely a plea for a division of labor in order to get urgent jobs done. As such, it affects only more or less applied economists, and it certainly offers no excuse for the failure of writers on so-called economic methodology to work out what is implied in the now almost universally accepted, though revolutionary, notion that our experience as a whole has one distinguishably economic aspect. Concerning how we are to express this notion, there is even greater agreement. Nearly all economists have made use of the concept of "scarcity" in some form or another.

We shall develop the notion of scarcity, which we shall borrow from them, in our own way. The points we stress will be different, and we shall have to subject to a careful consideration some which would seem worthy only of passing mention to a practical economist.

We shall begin by considering an event which everybody would agree had "something decidedly economic" about it, namely, the buying of a book. This is the kind of experience in which even the man in the street is compelled to recognize some "economic factor." The impecunious undergraduate, seduced into forgetting this by those alluring little notices offering credit, sooner or later has this fact painfully brought home to him. But what exactly is it about buying a book which is "economic"? At first sight, one might incline towards the view that one could simply say, "Why, the whole matter is an economic transaction." If it were then asked, "What is the range of the economic field?" one might think it enough to reply, "The whole field of buying and selling—of getting a living—of producing and exchanging 'material goods.'" But a very little reflection will show that this is too crude a view. In fact these various criteria of "being economic" are far from co-extensive.

When the undergraduate grasped the book, he certainly held in his hand the kind of entity which many philosophers would call a "material object." But if any books—or anything else, for that matter—are "material objects," all the books in the bookshop were certainly equally so. But the undergraduate offered his money—or more likely his I.O.U.—for *The Concept of Mind* and if, upon opening the parcel in his rooms, he discovered instead some new edition of the works of René Descartes, which we will suppose had just been produced by the same publishers and got up so as to possess almost identical physical qualities, this latter similarity would not prevent him from being grievously dissatisfied. He would return to the bookshop and insist upon an exchange, which we know would be granted. Thus even our commercial society realizes that one suffers an economic loss through having the philosophy of Descartes fobbed off on him. The "good" at issue in this economic transaction, in fact, was not distinguished by being "material."

In any case, if we pin our faith to the contention that it is the exchange, the lack, the acquiring, of "material" goods which makes a certain sphere of things "economic," we shall find this impossible to square with other popular views of the economic field. For instance, it is true that the book was bought and sold, but even if we take the extremely paradoxical view that the "economic good" which the undergraduate acquired in buying a book of philosophy can helpfully be called "material," we must face the fact that in an enormous number of purchases and sales nothing passes from hand to hand at all. Almost all personal services fall into this latter class.

Even the apparently promising criterion of "being bought and sold" will not hold water. There are two forms of this view, the truly naïve one being that the economic field is limited to *actual* purchases and sales. This leads to amusing results. For example, if in wartime some thousands of women who used to devote themselves to housework, for which they were not paid, allow their houses to get dirty while they work in war factories, for which they are paid, this theory would lead to the conclusion that there was a sudden violent rise, both in "economic activity" and in something called "economic wealth."

The more sophisticated notion is that the economic field includes all activities and experiences which either are *or could be* "brought into relation with the measuring rod of money." Yet this only makes matters worse. It is rather a tall order to say what activities *could not,* in any society, be "brought into" this relation; the whole notion is hopelessly vague.

But there is a much more radical weakness underlying all these more or less popular attempts to tie down the exact nature of "the economic." They all try to cut off a certain "section" of everyday life and say, "Within this everything is economic, and outside of it nothing is." But the criteria for marking off this section are so weak that one may well ask whether this "peculiarly economic" something is not after all a mirage? We may admit that the word "economic" has a clear enough sense to make possible its satisfactory use in the ordinary affairs of life, but we may still feel that it would not stand up to a philosophical analysis. This would be a mistake, however, both about the strengths and weaknesses of ordinary usage and about the subject matter of economic analysis. One can derive from a consideration of our ordinary ways of speaking an account of the economic aspect of experience which is remarkably precise and accurate. It has some shortcomings, but, as we shall see in due course, these only become serious when one wants to make certain statements of a very high degree of generality. The trouble about our ordinary speech is that it contains many usages which are inconsistent with those from which we can derive this account of the economic aspect of experience.

The trouble is certainly *not* that there is no clearly distinguishable aspect of our experience which can be validly said to be "economic": the undergraduate, who is now deep in *The Concept of Mind,* is rudely interrupted by the arrival of bills from a number of different bookshops, and reflects ruefully that there does indeed seem to be something vividly "economic" about things. He had intended soon to make a number of further purchases; now he sees that in order to retain even the books which he has he must forgo this.

Let us go back to the original purchase and see what it is that gives it the character which ordinary people recognize as economic, but find so difficult to define. We may be able to show that this simple series of events in a bookshop has an element in common with a number of the deepest and most subtle experiences which human beings ever have.

We should ordinarily feel quite correct in describing what took place in the bookshop as "an economic transaction," or "an economic action." We are accustomed to speak of "economic activities," "economic experiences," "economic life," "economic values," "economic decisions," "economic welfare," "economic losses and gains," "economic policy," "economic causes," "economic motives," "economic interests," "the economic sphere," and, of course, "economic man." If we consider critically sentences in which these

[16]

and similar expressions occur, we shall find that they all involve, to a greater or less extent on different occasions and in different contexts, the assumption that there is some *part* of our experience which it is appropriate to call economic, taken as a whole.

People would certainly normally call what took place in the bookshop "an economic transaction." Yet it would be possible to convince them that what took place had a number of aspects which it would not really be appropriate to call "economic" in any sense. The young man may have bought the book for examination purposes, and some people might try to hold that this was what they would call an "economic motive." But suppose he bought it out of a disinterested desire to learn the truth; one could hardly call this aspect of the matter economic. Even the granting of the I.O.U. is not exclusively economic; a student of comparative law could point out that the manner of this would differ in communities at different places and times; the matter has a legal aspect. Again, the young man leaning forward and eagerly holding out his book, the cover flashing in the dim light, seems, to the passing artist, to provide the material for a perfect picture. But these are only a few aspects chosen at random, out of the infinite number which might be distinguished in any concrete action.

If we are to trace the economic something in the scene in the bookshop, or in any other experience for that matter, we cannot talk as if the buying of a book, or any other activity, were "economic" as a whole. We must reject the implication which may appear to underlie many common expressions that there are such exclusively economic activities. If we fail to do this, we leave ourselves open to a series of easy but fallacious proofs that the word "economic" has no precise sense; if we say of some action simply that it is an economic one, it will inevitably be replied by specialists in different fields: "No, sir, it is a legal one," "Absurd, sir; its real significance is sociological," and so forth.

There is, however, one aspect of the young man's action which it is valid to call economic. He really wanted *The Concept of Mind,* but he also wanted dozens of other books. Yet, despite his unduly rosy views about his credit, he knew he was *limited* to one more book. The choice had to be made. But the necessity of choosing gave him an acute feeling of limitation; he felt bitterly, at this moment, how his extreme lack of means was preventing him from leading the life he would have liked to lead. He made the purchase which he thought would best economize what means he had.

Let us consider a number of other happenings in the life of this young man, choose incidents which appear to have as little in common as possible, both with the buying of a book and with each other, so as to bring into relief one of the few elements which is common to them all.

This young man, like other undergraduates, has as his ruling passion a vividly felt, if ill thought out, desire to discover what used to be called "the best life for man," and to follow this as far as possible. Being

[18]

young, this is not always uppermost in his thoughts; but it is an inveterate disposition, and he is still young enough to take it seriously. At times he is tormented by a positive sense of guilt at his intense, though inexplicable, awareness that he is "making little or no headway." He feels as one does in a nightmare when, having been given some impossible task, one accepts it unquestioningly as an obligation to fulfill. It is as if he were on trial before a court whose amazing and apparently quite unreasonable demands he could never satisfy, yet whose authority, much as he might rave against it, was incontestable. He is like that ever-recurring figure of myth and fairy-tale who is condemned to empty a lake with a tailor's thimble.

Now, in the light of this, look at those other incidents in his life which we promised to compare with the buying of the book.

To begin with, he has decided to get himself cheap lodgings, the cheapest he can find, in order to have more ready money for other things. This eases the situation about books, which he regards as vital to him; but, on the other hand, it introduces new and different factors into his life. He finds himself the possessor of a huge room full of great spotted mirrors; a room surrounded by a vivid life apparently completely hostile to his own. In the beginning he had felt that it would be worth trying to live cheaply so as to be able to acquire more of what he feels he needs for his development. But as time goes on, he is compelled to admit that the multitude of little irritations and oppressions

[19]

which perpetually steal in upon him have accumulated into what seems like a solid wall between him and the daylight.

He now feels that his choice was a wrong one; he compares "going without" the books and other things he wanted with "enduring" the new hostile atmosphere. There are few respects in which a cheap lodging house can be compared to a shelf of books on philosophy, yet the young man is able to find one common factor: he feels that he can assert that the "lack" of a sympathetic atmosphere is more "restricting" to him than a certain "lack" of books.

He finds on reflection that he can make the same kind of statement about the lack of sleep; staying up late at night enables him to get more work done, but after a certain point he finds that it is making him flag during the day. Thus he can compare "lack" of time to work and "lack" of efficiency when working, and finds himself trying to evaluate the relative effects of the two in "limiting" the extent to which he attains his object.

When he thinks the matter over he sees that there is a striking similarity between the questions he is asking himself about the "lack" of books, decent surroundings, time and energy, and another set of questions about which he is often worried. When he tries to paint he is forced to face the fact that his technique is "deficient"; again, he is honest enough to recognize that his English style is seriously "wanting." Ought he to try to develop both? If he takes this decision he runs the risk of never getting beyond mediocrity in either field. Would he "gain" more by devoting his "available resources" to one or other? But both his art and his writing seem to him like parts of himself which are trying to grow; to give up one of them is like agreeing to an amputation in order to save one's life. Gerard Manley Hopkins, believing at one time that his religious vocation required him to renounce the life of a poet, must surely have felt like this.

The young man suddenly realizes that he is making a very remarkable kind of comparison; he is first picturing to himself a whole delicate pattern of interwoven choices which gives a picture of one kind of life, then contrasting this with a picture which results from a divergent set of choices, and trying to decide which of these patterns he should adopt in order to "free" himself as much as possible from everything that would "restrict" his attainment of the end which dominates his thought. This choice seems to have something in common with the choice he made in the bookshop; he seems to be making the same kind of "evaluation" of two alternatives, one of which must be renounced.

Yet can this be? The two sets of alternatives are so vastly different. In the first case, it seemed just a matter of one book against another, or of one book against a fraction of the week's rent; in the second case it is a matter of "comparing"—in this peculiar mode of comparison which we are examining—one whole subtle pattern of life against another. Must we say that while the first comparison has meaning, the second cannot have?

It might be objected: "There is an economic aspect to an activity like buying a book; furthermore, many

common experiences have such an 'aspect.' " Nevertheless, there is only a doubtful analogy between the economic aspect of certain everyday experiences and the
supposedly similar "aspect" which you discern in certain very subtle experiences of quite a different order.
Surely the truth in popular expressions about the "economic part" of experience is that, while even this part
is far from wholly economic, only this part has *any*
economic aspect.

Yet when one recalls what the first comparison involved, it turns out not to be simpler than the second,
because what was at issue in the first comparison was
not just some simple good called a book versus another
simple good called lodgings; it was a chance to read the
philosophy of Professor Ryle versus the atmosphere of
a cheaper lodging-house. Likewise, the young man's
behavior makes it quite clear that he, at any rate, was
acting upon the assumption, conscious or not, that
there was some sense of "loss" in which it could be as-
serted unequivocally that his giving up either painting
or writing would cause him to suffer a loss in this sense.
If the sense in which he could say that he would lose by
giving up painting has only a doubtful analogical similarity to the sense in which he could say that he would
lose by giving up writing, then both his agitation and
his final decision are inexplicable, for there was nothing comparable to evaluate and to decide upon. Yet all
great literature is full of vivid descriptions of just such
evaluations and decisions.

Rather than suggest that some of the most vivid and

widely acknowledged of human experiences are based upon illusory issues and imaginary conflicts, let us consider whether the difficulties in understanding the matter may not simply be due to the inadequacy of our expression.

In what sense can the young man be said to have compared even one book with another? The *Concept of Mind* is not to him a white object of a certain size; it is a source of the philosophy of Mr. Ryle. This other larger object is a source of knowledge about Mrs. Beeton's views on household management. Was it not because these two were comparable, in some sense, and by comparing them, or weighing them against one another, that the undergraduate rejected Mrs. Beeton and chose Mr. Ryle? Did he not weigh Mr. Ryle's philosophy against the possibility of having to move into cheaper lodgings? These comparisons are of the same type as the comparison of the relative limitations involved in giving up writing or painting.

It is no more easy to give a statement of what is economic in buying a book than it is to describe the same element in choices whose subject-matter is taken from the subtlest of experiences. How *can* one compare the *Moonlight Sonata* and Gorgonzola cheese? Yet many a man stands undecided, chooses, and forgoes a record of the one for a pound of the other.

It boils down to this: what is economic in any experience lies in its effect upon the end or ends which a person is then, more or less consciously, pursuing. There is nothing economic about the end as such;

nothing is economic in itself. It is as if we were to say that something is perceived apart from a perceiver, or painful apart from some being who suffers.

Therefore, when anything needed for the achievement of an end—anything from a book to a favorable atmosphere—is insufficient for the end's attainment, it may stand as a term in the economic relation of scarcity. To our young man, books are scarce, time is scarce, talent is scarce, all the myriad elements of which an encouraging atmosphere consists are scarce, and much, much else is scarce besides. He cannot compare any of these things directly, but he may be aware of the effect upon him—or some of it at any rate—and he may try to act to minimize this detrimental effect. In other words, he may economize.

The dripping of unnumbered drops gradually wears away the stone; the lightly-falling snowflakes build up into a drift whose weight breaks down the roof; the individual instances of scarcity do not combine with one another as the snowflakes do, yet one cannot say for this reason that there is no cumulative effect. The multitude of differently colored pieces in a kaleidoscope, no matter how they fall, do not blend with one another, yet a total pattern results; the multitude of different instances of scarcity may not blend, but their pattern may be seen as the economic aspect of a person's situation. Reviewing in imagination all the instances of scarcity which affect a person, we may refer to all these summarily as "the scarcity"—in a universal or complete sense—affecting him.

This will prove a very convenient shorthand, but of

course adopting it involves turning "scarcity" into a technical term. And all these metaphors of drops, and snowflakes, and colored pieces are dangerous: we must not get into the way of thinking of scarcity as some sort of peculiar entity that exists in its own right, a sort of "stuff"—to do this would be to re-introduce, in a refined form, all these fallaciously "material" attitudes towards the subject matter of economics which we have followed recent economists in rejecting.

There have been many attempts to describe the total effect of scarcity upon a person. In some of the novels of Virginia Woolf, for instance, her precise imagery shows one little colored piece after another flash into place in each kaleidoscopic pattern. All the delicate incidents, whose economic aspect goes to make up the scarcity which dooms each individual, fall neatly into place. Her technique allows her to evaluate correctly some subtle instances of scarcity which may affect children deeply, but which, when seen from the point of view of a grown-up, may seem a mere nothing. Mrs. Ramsay has just finished reading to the boy James:

"And that's the end," she said, and she saw in his eyes, as the interest of the story died away in them, something else take its place; something wondering, pale, like the reflection of a light, which at once made him gaze and marvel. Turning, she looked across the bay, and there, sure enough, coming regularly across the waves first two quick strokes and then one long steady stroke, was the light of the Lighthouse. It had been lit.
In a moment he would ask her, "Are we going to the Lighthouse?" And she would have to say, "No: not tomorrow; your father says not." Happily, Mildred came in to fetch them, and the bustle distracted them. But he

kept looking back over his shoulder as Mildred carried him out, and she was certain that he was thinking, we are not going to the Lighthouse tomorrow; and she thought, he will remember that all his life.*

And years later, when Mrs. Ramsay is dead, and his father finally organizes a trip to the Lighthouse, James reflects:

> Suppose then that as a child sitting helpless in a perambulator, or on some one's knee, he had seen a waggon crush ignorantly and innocently, some one's foot? Suppose he had seen the foot first, in the grass, smooth, and whole; then the wheel; and the same foot, purple, crushed. But the wheel was innocent. So now, when his father came striding down the passage knocking them up early in the morning to go to the Lighthouse down it came over his foot, over Cam's foot, over anybody's foot. One sat and watched it.†

And in a later novel also the wagon begins to roll. The theme recurs; Neville uses an hour of solitude to try to recover, by standing on the same stair halfway up the landing, from the shock he felt on overhearing there the cook's account of the dead man:

> He was found with his throat cut. The apple-tree leaves became fixed in the sky; the moon glared; I was unable to lift my foot up the stair. . . . I shall call this stricture, this rigidity, 'death among the apple trees' for ever. There were the floating, pale-grey clouds; and the immitigable tree; the implacable tree with its greaved silver bark. The ripple of my life was unavailing. I was

* Virginia Woolf, *To the Lighthouse*, Harbrace Modern Classics ed. (New York: Harcourt, Brace & Co., 1927), pp. 94-95. Copyright © 1927 by Harcourt, Brace & Co., Inc., renewed 1955 by Leonard Woolf; reprinted by permission of the publisher.
† Ibid., p. 275.

unable to pass by. There was an obstacle. 'I cannot pass
this unintelligible obstacle,' I said. And the others passed
on. But we are doomed, all of us by the apple trees, by
the immitigable tree which we cannot pass.*

To look for a moment at a humbler life: a reed
stood waving, alive in the river water, but now someone has torn it up, stripped and notched it, depriving
it of life that it might be the instrument of his own
power to pipe back the day:

> The sun on the hill forgot to die,
> The lilies revived, and the dragon-fly
> Came back to dream on the river.
> Yet half a beast is the great god Pan
> To laugh as he sits by the river;
> The true gods sigh for the cost and pain,
> For the reed which grows never more again
> As a reed with the reeds by the river.†

Baudelaire has an image which expresses well how
the possession of poetic greatness, when one is deprived
of an atmosphere in which it can live and move, may
itself be the cause of one's greatest limitation—as the
wings of the albatross are a mere impediment when it
lies on the deck of a ship:

> Le Poëte est semblable au prince des nuées
> Qui hante la tempête et se rit de l'archer;
> Exilé sur le sol au milieu des huées,
> Ses ailes de géant l'empêchent de marcher.

* Virginia Woolf, *The Waves*, Harvest Book 37 (New York: Harcourt,
Brace and Co.), p. 191. Copyright © 1931 by Harcourt, Brace and Co.,
Inc., renewed 1959 by Leonard Woolf; reprinted by permission of the
publisher.
† From "The Musical Instrument" by Elizabeth Barrett Browning.

I now want to consider a couple of accounts of the situation when we feel, as we sometimes do, that we are faced with a choice between two whole patterns of life, and the cost of choosing one is giving up the other.

Very often, no doubt, closer examination of our situation would reveal that we had been mistaken, either in imagining that the two sorts of life really were incompatible, or in failing to see that there was some third alternative. But we cannot affirm offhand that such choices between whole patterns of living are never meaningful. In any case, once a person has chosen, deciding upon the end which he is going to pursue, we may take his choice as given for the purpose of a purely economic analysis of the various effects of scarcity upon the achievement of the chosen end. Among such instances of scarcity will be some which may appear rather startling; those elements in his experience which would favor the pattern of life which he has rejected may not be merely useless to him now —they may be a positive hindrance. They thus count as instances of economic scarcity.*

There are many passages in the *Confessions* where one feels Augustine's desperate struggle to decide between two whole patterns of life which seem to him to be quite irreconcilable. He certainly felt, as Kierkegaard was later to feel, that there are certain opposites which cannot be synthesized. I do not want to lay stress

* This use of the concept of scarcity, while perfectly good in contemporary economics, involves departing from the ordinary use of the word "scarce."

on the question of whether Augustine was right as to the absoluteness of the particular "either/or" he was considering; my interest is in pointing out the complexity of the range of "deprivations" which he felt were at stake. It is interesting to note that even long after he had made his choice he felt conscious of a delicate pattern of excluded alternatives; he draws up an amazingly detailed inventory of these at the close of the tenth book of the "Confessions." He gives us such accounts as these of the instances of scarcity to which he regards himself as still subject:

> There yet live in my memory . . . the images of such things, as my ill custom there fixed; which haunt me, strengthless when I am awake: but in sleep, not only so as to give pleasure, but even to obtain assent, and what is very like reality. Yea, so far prevails the illusion of the image, in my soul and in my flesh, that, when asleep, false visions persuade to that which when waking, the true cannot. . . .

> With the allurements of smells, I am not much concerned. When absent, I do not miss them; when present I do not refuse them; yet ever ready to be without them. So I seem to myself; perchance I am deceived. . . .

> The delights of the ear, had more firmly entangled and subdued me; but thou didst loosen, and free me. . . .

> There remain the pleasures of these eyes of my flesh. . . . The eyes love fair and varied forms, and bright and soft colours. Let not these occupy my soul; let God rather occupy it. . . . For this queen of colours, the light, bathing all which we behold, wherever I am through the day, gliding by me in varied forms, soothes me when engaged on other things, and not observing it. And so strongly doth it entwine itself, that if it be sud-

denly withdrawn, it is with longing sought for, and if
absent long, saddeneth the mind. . . .*

The pattern chosen by Clifford Chatterley has something in common with Augustine's—he was enough of
a Platonist for this to be true. But consider the point
of view of someone who, like Constance, makes the op-
posite choice. They are discussing the myth of the two-
horse chariot of the soul from the *Phaedrus,* and the
novel that follows is concerned largely with elaborating
the consequences of their different views about Plato's
tri-partite division of the soul. Constance has a very
different view from Clifford as to the rights and needs
of the "black horse":

> "Don't you think it's rather cruel, the way Socrates
> drives his black horse—jerking him back till his mouth
> and tongue are full of blood, and bruising his haunches?
> Don't you think one could manage a horse better than
> that?" . . .
> "Perhaps not a vicious horse," he said. . . .
> She had felt in herself a deep indifference to Clifford's
> immortality and Clifford's heaven of the pure abstrac-
> tion. . . . And latterly it had begun to seem a certain
> prison: Like the white-hot steel walls of a Poe story. She
> hated it, this heaven of pure justice and truth. She felt
> herself being insidiously, insufferably bullied by him in
> the name of this pure heaven of justice. She felt that
> Plato, exalting the heaven of pure justice, did it by
> committing all the time one horrible injustice. He was
> unjust to the black horse. . . .
> . . . Clifford bullied her, not by obvious compulsion,
> but by insidious negation. Some part of her soul he just

* Edward B. Pusey, trans. *The Confessions of Saint Augustine* (New
York: Pocket Books, Inc., 1957), pp. 197-203.

absolutely ignored, he killed it by not allowing its existence. As one might kill a person by withdrawing all the air from them.*

As one might kill a person by withdrawing all the air from them . . . to see this being done—to see someone dying slowly for want, as it were, of some constituent of the air a human being needs to breathe —to be unable to say exactly what, yet know intuitively what is happening, and that nobody intends this death or is even aware that it is taking place before their eyes; to watch helplessly the slow dying of such an expiring spirit is to be acquainted with scarcity. Once seen, it is never forgotten.

Let us consider a young man whom every circumstance of time and place and feeling had combined to make most receptive to the movement of half hidden things. The first soft summer green had come to the austere grey eighteenth century squares of Trinity; in the night the reading room was a dim world hung with still green eyes, and when he came out Front Square was full of memory and warm mellow silence. It was impossible to believe that it was in the middle of a modern city: "The College of the Holy and Undivided Trinity, *near* Dublin" . . . that was how the description would be translated and the "near" still seemed exactly right. Silent and bat-like, officers of an ancient Society, gowned and in white tie and tails, slipped over the cobbles to a meeting of the Hist. Dark grey shapes

* D. H. Lawrence, *The First Lady Chatterley*, pp. 48-53. Copyright © 1944 by The Dial Press, Inc., used with the permission of the publisher.

came out of the shadows thrown by old walls. If one were young and warmly responsive to the spirits that hung about the place, ideas grew to be a consuming silent fever in the blood. But he was at that time just a young undergraduate, with no formed concepts of his own; above all he had the undergraduate's typical sense of the recent loss of old familiar beliefs, of deep uncertainty, of undirected, dammed up energy.

There was an old house in Dublin. In itself it was an anomaly. One walked in right off a street, through quiet rooms, and out all at once into an old rambling garden that might have been buried deep in the country, miles from anywhere. It must have been a country garden once, but the city had flowed round it— closing it in but leaving it intact—passed it and spread far beyond. One came there off a dusty noisy street, but once inside one was deep in silence and a place where time had paused, a place where it was possible to meet the past again. The family who lived there were old friends of his parents. They and their parents had been friends when old country places that are now gone or fading from memory stood in splendor at the end of long drives lined with the dark green and the rich flower of the rhododendrons.

A childhood friend of his was living in this old house and with these people—exactly why or in what role he did not know—but anyway she had turned up again as unexplained as always, just as she had vanished one summer years before. When he learned of her reappearance from some casual remark, and that he would see her the next time he dropped in for tea—it seemed somehow impossible—images rushed up from the past and gave him no peace.

He had been a young boy when he saw her last, and he could not distinguish her from the sunlight of the spring; the golden hair fell down her back, a wavering trail of moving light following her among those shadows of the woods that were the darkest places in their world. He did not know what to call his feelings then. She was utterly entangled in his consciousness with all the things that open and look upwards towards the sky in April. Even rain, when it came then, was just the overflowing of joy. Clear bright water raced through those days, falling shining over the grey stones and stirring the green darkness of the moss; those days wound gaily down by mountain ways through silent pines and into the bold buttercup yellow of the noonday fields. Playing over the lawns, children's laughter broke up the silence that surrounds old eight-foot walls that had been built to withstand the cannon shot of a different siege. Through it all ran a gay golden thread, a spell woven laughingly by fingers and eyes that danced through the play of their work. He saw it all again. It was like coming on an old tapestry, found in a dusty attic where children once would make believe that they were medieval gallants. All gone dull, but for one golden thread.

She had reappeared—suddenly, and without explanation, as she had once gone—in the hidden garden of that old silent house in Dublin. How she had come to be there was obscure—she was in no way obviously related to the Doctor or his wife, or to the old lady, the

Doctor's mother. She was living there, but how or why she was there he could not pin down—there was something very graceful and charming about these people which nevertheless produced a certain reserve, prevented quite effectively one's thinking of asking questions. As far as he could discover she was not a niece or a second cousin or anything so obvious as that. They never spoke about her background. Nor did she, for that matter, except once jokingly, and then only by implication: she corrected him laughingly for mispronouncing her name, telling him it had originally been Norman French. There was a little gentle pride of the past in her attitude towards her name.

She spent most of her time looking after the old lady, but again she was certainly not simply a paid companion—he was quite sure she wasn't paid a salary, and it was rumored that since the Doctor and his wife had no children she would one day inherit anything that did not go to one or two nieces. And, as he was to have reason to discover, she had none of a companion's regular hours, nor clearly stated days when she was free. But neither was she an adopted daughter. People do not leave one in any doubt about their adopted children: they treat them like any other children and if there is anything that one does not discover till later it is the fact that they were adopted. Yet it was said that they were going to leave her most of what they had. She was a sort of changeling.

He did not know quite what he had expected to find when he first went to that old house, in answer to a formal invitation, knowing that she would be there, that he would see her again for the first time in years, for the first time since those golden days. It was a garden party in high midsummer, and the sun shone favorably down on well-kept lawns and glinted through the green twined lattice work by little walks. People rattled teacups in the shade of still trees and talked about the Horse Show. How would she be? What would she have become? To what glorious fulfillment? As he looked about him he was ashamed, thinking that everyone must surely sense what he was waiting for.

And then he saw her in the distance, before she had yet seen him, and in an instant knew that all the time he had been watching for her and trying not to let it show he had been worrying for nothing: they did not think of her as someone who would be watched or much noticed. And she moved about among them like an attendant, carefully domesticated sprite, utterly unaware that anyone could be staring at her. Then she saw him and walked over with outstretched hand and a light smiling greeting as if she had last seen him a few days before, and nothing had passed since that was worth his comment.

All around him people were talking gaily, but he was suddenly utterly alone: there was something in that garden that took him by the throat while leaving everyone else quite untouched and unaware of its existence. She seemed to him as if she were walking in some sort of sleep, bound in a trance that drained away all her vivid powers of life, leaving barely movement and trivial speech. He watched her fascinated, trying to fathom something of the nature of the spell. Everything that he could see or sense about her as she revealed herself to him now was flatly inconsistent with each and every golden possibility she had once so unmistakably shown. It was no use pointing to the triviality of the occasion, and the trying social circumstances of such a gathering—in the old days she would have shone through such petty things. The impression grew with every moment in her presence.

As he watched her she was handing a teacup to a red-faced old gentleman who stood bowlegged from the saddle, bowing abruptly as he took the cup. Of course, physically she had aged—but it was not in the way of a reasonable growth and maturing, even riper flowering: it was all visibly a draining away, a growing dim. The lights in her hair and eyes had been put out. Her hair was short now—its golden abundance had all been cut away—though not, somehow, to grant her a grownup glory; simply shorn away; one felt only an absence. There was a web of little lines about her eyes and mouth, but they were not the strong traces of lived joy and sorrow—just a withering. A sedentary life had taken the lightness from her step and stolen the lissome woodland grace of movement. And whoever was responsible for her clothes was certainly not helping—could they be all her own idea? They were expensive, well cut, and in perfect taste. But there was nothing young about them. They were either an imprisonment or a sign of surrender to some unseen forces, the truce flags of a dying hope. With all this she had acquired a set, controlled look.

She was no longer a girl to leave you breathless on a summer day. People accepted teacups from her. They hardly looked up, murmured casual thanks. Everyone thought she was such a nice kind girl—it was so lucky for the old lady that she was there. How could they be so blind? Yet they were right, as far as concrete actuality went. All the rest was potential—if it was even that: he could not be sure that even the possibility was left. At moments he was sure he had caught a glimpse of it, trembling shyly on the edge of actuality, simply never having had what would draw it out into full glorious flower. He could have sworn it was there—he could see it. Standing as he did himself on the edge of childhood, still able now and then for an enchanted moment to see back into all those hidden forgotten places as well as forward into the grownup day, he could see her life dynamically, feel again the opening bud of her youth and carry it forward in his imagination to the full bloom that should be before him now. He could see childhood dying unfulfilled in her face, lingering into what had already become evening.

But there was still possibility. Or was there? Suddenly, as he looked on fascinated, it all seemed to fall away under him, everything was plunged into utter triviality, and he desperately searched her face and form for any trace—however slight—that would betray a sign of life. She was saying polite goodbyes,

everything was breaking up; he pulled himself together and took his leave.

It was cool and still when he left, but he could draw
no peace from the silence of twilight. He had begun a
long and lonely journey. He was determined to try to
reach and reawaken in her the possibilities he had once
seen so brightly—if any trace of them could still be
found.

From then on he accepted every invitation that
might give him a chance to meet her. It did not seem to
be noticed that quite often they were to be seen slightly
apart, talking together. He quickly found that her
mind, as they wandered about some quiet garden and
she played in fancy over all those old things they had
shared, still showed little traces of its childhood grace
—traces that in the context of her life now had all the
more haunting magic. But their talk was like the playing of some old courtly game in which one never
referred to what was really important. The things he
really wanted to know about her he was quite unable
to ask. And what he wanted to say to her, what he
wanted to make her face, he could not: he had not the
maturity to know how to make her lay aside the masks
with grace, and was too sensitive to attempt it crudely.

And it was very difficult to manage to spend much
time really alone with her. The fact that she was some
years the elder, together with his youth, did not make
the approach any easier. At last he found what seemed
an excellent excuse: he had a small sailing boat in those
days, which was his pride and joy, and he let fall the

suggestion that she might like to come out on it. She rose immediately to this—she was overwhelmed, for a few moments there was real animation—and since the family had no objection and even supported the idea, a day was fixed.

When the day came it was a steady downpour. The sea has its glories even in foul weather, but this was the sort of day when the sky is an even grey and there is almost no wind and it just rains. Yet she insisted on going out—it meant that much to her.

As they drifted through this grey world she discovered little gleaming lights he had not seen in sea and sky, and the hope of a lift, and following them the boat glided forward over quicksilver into a freshening air. It was an astounding day; he felt as if she had physically drawn the sun out. Wild hopes took flight on impossible wings.

They died the moment he tried to ask her out again: after that first sail he had been sure there would be no great effort needed to persuade her to come out often, but it was not so. Try as he might she could not be enticed—or rather it could not somehow be arranged for her to go out with him more than once or twice again that summer. Every effort he made met with a strange indefinable resistance. She seemed to find it impossible to get away on her own. He could never discover the exact nature of this inability, but it was palpably there, and it could in no way be overcome. There were always good excuses made, and these usually involved the conveniences of the old lady, or of the whole household, but since they could hardly have objected to her having some time to herself, he could not help suspecting that she was creating part of the difficulty herself. Yet he knew how she had loved it—even at its worst—on the water, and he knew she did not dislike his company. It was as if she somehow could not bear often sallying out, facing the grownup world outside, on her own. And on the few rare occasions when they were actually alone for most of a day, out on the cool water of the bay, the intensity of it was too much for him, and the spell and the sea tied his tongue, and he could not find anything to say, and they spoke lightly of the boat and of the sea.

It was when his efforts to be alone with her and learn about her directly from her own lips failed that he began to question those who had seen something of the family in the years between her childhood and the present. Curiously little, however, seemed to be known. Even the most obviously public facts—whether, for instance, she had ever been engaged—were unknown. He wondered if she had ever had a lover. What he did know was that no man had been enough to her, or had had the chance, to draw her out so that the potencies he had felt so strongly must become, and stay, fully actual. Something could well have begun—as she had in so many ways—to flower. But in order for those potentialities not to be stifled, something quite other than a man might have been needed, and this having been lacking to her, perhaps she could never draw any man in the right way. By the time he had met her again at the garden party the only sort of man who could possibly have lifted her bodily out of the snow in which she was so quietly and resignedly going to sleep would have had to be someone fully mature and in command of his powers, not a mere youth.

Yet something whose roots he was very far from understanding stirred strongly in him, making him want desperately to be able to fight for her life. His youth and inexperience held him powerless—someone much older might not have known where to turn. He could do absolutely nothing. He had never known such frustration, such absolute helplessness. Unable to act, without anybody to whom he could possibly have talked—had he been able to formulate the situation—he was driven in upon his own thoughts. He discovered, tempered under such pressure, a hitherto unsuspected power: not the warm active power to help for which he sought so anxiously, but something quite different—a power to understand and begin to see, even where there was no self-delusion that thus abstractly seeing could ever let him aid her.

His deepest, most all-pervading feeling about her was the tormenting, ever-present sense of unfulfilled potentiality—that she was potentially something which she had never become. He could remember so well how she had been once—the bright vision swept up quite unbidden to torment him, full of the laughing promise of the spring. What she had become was before his eyes every time they met. There was some sense of "could" in which she could have been so much more—even if he could not say exactly all the various subtle forms this "more" might have taken. But what exactly does it mean to say of people that they are potentially much more than they are? Is one claiming that appearances are deceptive, and that the people at the garden party did not see the real girl? Surely they saw precisely the real girl, just what in fact was actually there to see. The warrant for their estimation was before their eyes. It was all his claims about her that stood in need of justification. Suppose he admitted that all the things that he still saw were traces that hinted at "What could have been"—possibilities that had never been fulfilled. He felt an intense sense of loss. But even this proved difficult to account for. It makes sense to lament the dead—something that actually existed, someone who was alive is no more; but does it make sense to mourn for human qualities that never came into being, that, after all, never were there? For something that never flowered? What sort of loss is implied in such sheer unfulfillment of human possibilities?

However hard the claim might be to express, he had no doubt of its terrible, inescapable validity: the effects of scarcity were no illusion, though one might never see the end of them. So much in her had been killed—for him and for everyone—through its dying in her. Even the bare possibility, he felt sure, had now gone. He had fought madly, as Kierkegaard puts it, for possibility:

> When one swoons people shout for water, *Eau de Cologne,* Hoffman's Drops; but when one is about to despair the cry is, Procure me possibility, procure possibility! Possibility is the only saving remedy; given a possibility and with that the desperate man breathes once more, he revives again; for without possibility a man cannot, as it were, draw breath.*

\* Walter Lowrie, trans. Søren Kierkegaard, *The Sickness unto Death,* Anchor ed. (Garden City, N.Y.: Doubleday & Company, Inc., 1954), p. 172.

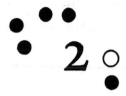

2

There is a kind of moral agony in which the consciousness of guilt and the sheer horror of those memories that come back to haunt us again and again seem to be merely different facets of the same inescapable truth. The query, "Ought I to be thus tormented by guilt, am I really to blame?" then seems sufficiently answered simply by glancing back for a moment over the shoulder at the ghostly faces of our past, where the mere sight of the wounds we have inflicted on others or upon ourselves seems to answer any possible question. The bare fact of what Oedipus had done—however unwittingly—was enough to drive him to his destruction, and Hamlet laments "I am myself indifferent honest, but yet I could accuse me of such things that it were better my mother had not borne me. . . ."

Yet we are all acquainted with situations which, however terrible, cannot be regarded as anyone's responsibility. Lives can be destroyed and souls can wither seemingly without anyone in particular to blame. The effects of scarcity can be distressing enough, as we have seen.

The vital point is that our horror at a happening

can never be our warrant for a certain type of moral judgment. The moment we see this we begin trying to divert the tide of guilt from the question "What has happened?" to the question "Is anyone to blame?"

We might overhear a conversation such as: "It was a terrible thing for her to do." "Can you blame her?" "Why not?" "Think of what she had been through—how could you expect her to be able to act differently?" "Yes, I suppose you're right. Still, it's a ghastly enough story anyway you look at it."

In this bit of dialogue there is an appeal to a distinction which will prove of crucial importance to the argument. It is a distinction which we constantly use in our day-to-day ethical discussions, without being able to give, or even needing, any account of what we are doing. In other important, but more complicated, circumstances, however, we commonly tend to become inconsistent, and our language reflects inconsistencies in sizing up the situation and encourages us to fall into further contradictions which a different way of expression might have prompted us to avoid.

Unfortunately, my analysis cannot be carried on simply by an examination of the contrast between the different ways in which we use ethical words and expressions, since part of my purpose is to point out that we do not possess *any* ethical words and expressions which are used solely with one of the two kinds of force which I want to distinguish. For convenience, I shall speak of the distinction as that between using ethical words and expressions in "ascribing" respon-

[46]

sibility, and using them in "appraising" states of affairs. I am giving "ascribing" and "appraising" special restricted meanings, but wherever these words appear in this book, they can be replaced by the detailed accounts which will be offered of the different sorts of ethical judgment at issue. In fact, the use of "ascribing" and "appraising" in this book seems to correspond closely to one of the ways in which each word is commonly used; but in any case, anyone who objects to my distinction between ascriptions and appraisals may interpret the distinction as being simply between say "A-type uses" and "B-type uses" of ethical words.

Crudely, we ascribe "responsibility" to a person whereas we appraise any number of things about him: his performance as Othello, his talent for oils, his involvements with women, his habit of being late, his addiction to drink or opium, his love of gambling, his reactions to his background, his whole state—without specifying for how much of this he is responsible. Furthermore we can appraise things other than people: the devastation produced down South by last year's hurricane, the climate of Ibiza, a Greek play, the administration of a British colony.

Yet ascriptions and appraisals are both instances of ethical uses of language: ascriptions both say that someone is responsible and convey an evaluation; appraisals evaluate a situation without assigning responsibility. There is a sense of ascription in which to ascribe responsibility is merely to claim, "He was responsible for that action," without attaching any praise or blame

[47]

for the action.* This, however, is not what I intend:
by an ascription I mean the sort of judgment which
both assigns responsibility and gives praise or blame.
Such a judgment is clearly ethical. On the other hand,
an appraisal in my sense is also an ethical use of language, but ascribes no responsibility, involves no praise
or blame. Some of the most ancient and typical of all
ethical utterances are of this type, for instance,
"Knowledge is a greater good than pleasure," "Pain
as such is evil."

Let us now examine the ways in which we normally
decide whether a putative ascription is warranted. Suppose someone asks, "How *could* he have told her something that was going to break her heart?" and the
hearer replies, "But don't you see he just didn't know
what it all meant to her—he didn't know what he was
giving away."

If the second speaker can establish his point beyond
dispute, then the first speaker will withdraw his putative ascription and make some other comment such
as, "Well, he's not to blame but I still wouldn't want
to be in his shoes."

A putative ascription will always be *withdrawn*
when the proper factual evidence is produced. If an
ethical judgment is held in abeyance pending the production of this sort of evidence, then it is not an appraisal, for an appraisal is not concerned with *how*

* See H. L. A. Hart, "The Ascription of Responsibility and Rights," in
A. G. N. Flew, ed., *Essays on Logic and Language*, First Series (New York:
Philosophical Library, Inc., 1951).

any state of affairs came about or with *who* is responsible, if anyone. On the other hand if a state of affairs
may be described as wholly due to any circumstance
for which no one is responsible, then an ethical judgment about this state of affairs cannot be an ascription,
or imply one.

It is important to see that this holds true, no matter
what the state of affairs is due to. This can be seen
quite simply if it is realized that an ascription will
always be withdrawn if someone can show that the
person was not responsible for the state at issue, irre-
spective of what sort of pressure forced it upon him.
We do not impute praise or blame to the results of
any circumstances affecting people, for which they
are not responsible; as soon as we suspect the existence
of such a mistake we withdraw any ascription we had
been prepared to make, pending a new judgment.

Thus ascriptions are what has been called *defeasible,*
in that they will be withdrawn upon production of the
relevant evidence. Unfortunately it has proved difficult
to formulate any general criteria for distinguishing between circumstances when it makes sense to blame,
and circumstances when it only makes sense to appraise. This is reflected in the fact that our ordinary
uses of ethical language often leave unclear whether
an ascription or an appraisal is intended: "That was
a disgusting way to behave!" Is this an ascription or an
appraisal?

It turns out, however, that all the circumstances
relevant to the defeat of putative ascriptions, where

[49]

somebody is known to have done something of which we disapprove, share the formal property of being what are described in the last chapter as instances of scarcity.

People recognize the more obvious instances of scarcity that arise through the usual stresses and strains of living, and insofar as they do recognize these instances of scarcity for what they are, people do not regard these deprivations as blameworthy. When we normally go astray is in dealing with the happenings in which we do not recognize anything economic. Here we are almost bound to attempt to ascribe responsibility for what are in fact only subtler instances of scarcity, and to miss subtle kinds of exonerating circumstances.

In ordinary language, words standing for long term character traits—dispositional terms like the names of abnormal mental conditions: kleptomania, dipsomania, nymphomania, and the like—are often used with an ascribing force, despite the fact that quite clearly having one of these traits of character is an instance of scarcity: "You lousy rummy," "She is a neurotic bitch," "You dirty little tramp." These utterances are all about long term dispositions, and they are certainly made blamingly. This sort of ascription might be justified by explicitly claiming that the present abnormal mental condition was in some sense wholly the result of past actions for which responsibility could be ascribed to the person. My present concern, however, is to point out that remarks about such mental conditions are often made ascribingly without it being clear that any long account of the way in which the condition was acquired is necessary if the ascription is to have any force.*

Consider remarks which might be made about any of the children in *The Waves*. Suppose someone says: "Neville was better when he was a child." Of what are we thinking when we make this kind of remark? Our thoughts might be something like this:

> Neville showed such signs of vivid life when he was young. You could see his bright imagination in everything he did or said. And yet, like all the other children he was gradually borne down. You could watch the gradual dulling of the sparkle, the dimming of the light, and we saw the disillusioned creature that he turned into.

The ordinary person might be ready to assert that in giving this kind of full description of Neville's character we had already described incidentally his moral condition. If the phrase "moral condition" is just an oddly formed appraisal phrase, fair enough. Of course, a full account of the economic aspect of Constance Chatterley's experiences would contain many statements which the ordinary person, overhearing them by chance, would take to be statements about what he would call her moral character. But this only means that he is using "moral" as an appraisal word. To describe immorality (intended as an ascribing word) as *due* to any instance of scarcity is like describing it as due to the measles.

The plausibility which this kind of mistake can have

---

* Mathematical economists may note what a complicated job constructing a formal model of a fully dynamic scarcity situation could be.

depends upon failing to see that all instances of scarcity are equally of the economic type. This failing prevents one's seeing that if he makes an ascription with respect to any one instance of scarcity, then he is committed to treating any other instance of scarcity in the same way. However, if this were admitted, it would soon become obvious that there were an enormous number of instances of scarcity which could not plausibly be treated in this way.

Thus people would not confuse a statement that someone lacked talent as a painter with ascriptions of responsibility, nor would they make this mistake if told that someone lacked good health or had deficient eyesight. But with most of the subtler instances of scarcity described towards the end of the last chapter people might not be so clear. Almost all the instances of scarcity described there are of a sort which constantly form the subject matter of what are intended to be ascriptions of responsibility. Yet, as we have seen, it makes as little sense to confuse such statements with ascription as it does in the case of any remark of the same type. If economic statements are logically different from ascriptions of responsibility, this holds for all of them indifferently. On the other hand, if we were to deny this distinction we should have to regard as blameworthy failures which it is obviously ridiculous to treat in this way. We should have to blame the sick for their illnesses, and the blind for being unable to see.

Need I stress, after all that has been said, that any attempt to ascribe where it only makes sense to appraise is not merely logically inappropriate, but grossly unjust as well?

At this point it may be said, "You are trying to narrow the area of moral responsibility. If your criteria were accepted much of what we now regard as blameworthy could no longer be held to be so. This could be a dangerous doctrine."

I reply: Can morality live and thrive upon unfair judgments and mistaken notions? Has not all genuine moral progress depended precisely upon the development of ever subtler ideas of responsibility, of just when it does and when it does not make sense to judge, and blame? Consider the development of humane legislation out of the primitive savagery of early law. Consider the influence of psychiatric medicine in forcing us to recognize as instances of scarcity what our grandparents would have regarded as the outcome of man's natural corruption. The concept of scarcity does not spring out of nowhere; it formalizes a whole tendency of thought which people are continually adopting in their approach to living.

Ignoring the significance and range of the effects of scarcity involves having an unwarrantedly rosy estimate of people's responsibility, and acting accordingly. It involves continually treating as blameworthy actions what are in fact the results of scarcity. And above all— since human nature instinctively rebels against such mistaken and unjustified judgments—it involves discrediting ethics. This is no small matter.

There are few topics with which young people today are as much concerned as they are with moral notions.

To be young today is to be desperately perplexed about how to act, and this state is then raw material for moral philosophy. But if there is one thing as intense as this ethical searching, it is the almost universal feeling that existing moral ideas "let one down," that they "don't work in practice," "don't fit our situation," and so on. Who has not had the experience of being in a situation where all the ethical notions one possesses say that one is deeply guilty, yet one dimly suspects that this is not really so, that the concepts that one was brought up with are not really coming to grips with the situation, that they are failing to account for some aspect of it which one has felt too vividly to be able to ignore, but which doesn't fit the pattern? There is always much suffering in this fight between inculcated moral convictions and the brute facts of experience, but the pain is the least of the damage which results. What is really disastrous is the way in which ethical thinking in itself becomes discredited, cast aside like some rocking horse from childhood that can carry one nowhere in the world of fact.

Something has now to be said about why it is that some of our everyday ethical expressions do not accurately reflect the distinction between ascribing and appraising. Do we not always use words like "moral," "responsible," "dutiful," in order to make what have here been called ascriptions?

It may be admitted that although all our usual ethical words are employed in making both ascriptions and appraisals, some are typically used for one or the other of these two tasks. Indeed it can be shown that there are a

few expressions which are so markedly adapted for one
or the other of these uses that it is tempting to say that
when they are used in the other way language suffers.
It is, for example, certainly true that words like
"moral," "obligatory," "culpable," "conscientious,"
"guilty," "praiseworthy," "wicked," "well-inten-
tioned," and the like are primarily used in making
ascriptions, whereas words like "fine," "noble,"
"tragic," "good," are primarily used in making appraisals.

Yet correct English sentences can be constructed in
which words like "moral" can be used in what are
clearly appraisals, but in which they are qualified by
other words whose point requires that the judgments
be ascriptions of responsibility. An instance of this is
offered in the following. Someone is discussing the
causes of delinquency: "By the time he was sixteen he
was already a person of completely vicious character
and it is not an exaggeration to say that you could find
nothing but blame for all his actions. I am certain that
his slum environment was totally responsible for his
behavior."

Is this merely an appraisal of a state of affairs, or does
some ascribing come in? Part of what is said in the
passage carries at least the strong suggestion that no
ascription would be warranted, yet in several places
the speaker so uses language as to imply that ascription
is possible. As language is currently used, one is often
subjected to this kind of uncertainty; expressions that
in all conscience are only entitled to be taken as appraisals often manage to gather around them the pe-

culiar sting of blame. Just because we are not clear
that there are two logically different types of ethical
judgment we might be making, we tend to slide from
one to the other.

Sometimes a single short sentence or one expression
is used to convey both an ascription and an appraisal,
telescoped together. This need not involve confusion
or error. The one sentence may express a complex
judgment. It may be a way of conveying both the points
to which the speaker wants to draw attention. When
someone says, "What a dreadful thing to do!" or
"God, that was a disgusting way to act!" he may be
both making an unfavorable appraisal of the state of
affairs and ascribing blame for it.

Trouble arises when similar expressions are used on
occasions when they could not legitimately be ex-
panded into both an appraisal and an ascription, because their familiar forms lead one to assume that they
have this combined force. Often our way of blaming
someone is to appraise unfavorably what has resulted
from his action, allowing the ascription of responsibility to be inferred: "Look what you've done!" Then
when all we are entitled to do is to appraise some result of the effects of scarcity, this normal implication of
guilt sticks to our habitual appraisal. The confusion
noted above in uses of words like "moral" probably
often arose in this way. Perhaps *"moral"* is not often
used with the intention of making only what I have
called an appraisal—although phrases like "moral condition" and "morals" probably are. What happens is
that people begin by using this word to make tele-

scoped appraisals plus ascriptions, and come to asso-
ciate its use with the making of certain familiar appraisals. They then pass to using the word wherever
they want to make such appraisals whether or not in
the particular case they would want to make any ascription if they considered the matter separately, or would
even claim that one could be made.

I have had to lean on the use of words like "blame,"
"praise," "responsibility," "guilt," to convey what I
wanted to say about the character of ascription. Although these words come as near as any to being used
only in the making of ascriptions, unfortunately, as
was mentioned earlier in the chapter, there are no
words in English which are used exclusively in this
way.

We can speak quite correctly of "praising" skilled
performances, where skill is due to endowment, or the
possession of special training—where, that is to say, we
cannot be making an ascription in praising. "Responsible" and "guilty" perhaps come nearest of all to what
is required, but both these words have at any rate one
use in which they are certainly not being employed to
make ascriptions. We often speak of someone as being
"guilty" of a wrong action, implying merely that he has
in fact done the action—whether through ignorance,
under the pressure of an obsession, or whatever. "Responsible" has also certain uses—among them the one
in which it is nearly synonymous with "in charge"—
in which it is at any rate not obviously being used
to make ascriptions. For a while, I considered the
possibility of using the word "imputation" instead of ascription and of making a distinction between

ethical judgments which involve making favorable or unfavorable imputations and those that do not. But it was pointed out to me that, strictly, we impute motives (usually bad ones!) rather than praise or blame as such. There is however one use of "imputing" which comes near to what I want—that in which we say of someone "His behavior was terrible but really no imputation can be made."

The lack of clear distinctions in our language between ascribing words and appraisal words would be much less serious if the nature of our experience was such as to draw our attention continually to the different sorts of force of these two kinds of ethical judgments. However, the subtle all-pervading effects of scarcity are such as to obscure continually the distinction between the blameworthy and the tragic. Guilt grows around certain actions like moss around stones. It is felt that to have done such an action is necessarily blameworthy—we are, as it were, soiled by having touched such things. Here conscience cries out "Look, I did it. Nothing you can say will ever take that away!"

But the conscience is confused in its claim. Real loss, real suffering, real horror, or some unforgettable violence to humanity—yours or another's—may have taken place. But this does not entail blame.

Apart from the effects of scarcity, our morality would show directly and unmistakably in what we achieved. But given that the effects are severe enough, there is no reason why someone who was quite blameless should not fail to attain almost anything, earning the unmerited contempt and condemnation of the world and—worst of all—bearing within his own heart the bitter pangs of failure. Sometimes we can virtually watch what someone could be, trembling on the edge of actuality, held back by some subtle lack. Thus the young man in the previous chapter watched the withering of the girl's possibilities, helpless to stop the approach of this death. No blame was to the point. But how clearly in this case the inapplicability of blame does not entail the avoidability of regret. One can free the innocent victims of scarcity from the agony of remorse, but this does not remove the grounds for regretting the loss. Those who died in the hurricane are on nobody's conscience, but this does not make their deaths any less regrettable. This is too often forgotten by those who confuse blame with regret. They feel that if one is to be really upset it must be because somebody is to blame. So their first thought is to look for a scapegoat, and if it becomes clear that one cannot be found they then sit back with a sigh of relief and say, "Oh well, no one was to blame, it couldn't be helped"—as if this took away all cause for sorrow.

One can consider a number of cases. There is the extreme case, where literally no blame can be ascribed: the heroine rushes on stage, shoots the hero dead—only someone has substituted a pistol that fires live shells, and the hero really is dead. How does she feel now? And how do we? We may even feel a certain oddness about using a verb like "shot"—that to say, "She shot him," is somehow to misdescribe the situation—even if we add a phrase like, "by accident," "by mistake" or "unintentionally." We feel that the unsuspected substitution of a real gun for a stage property needs to be marked by some stronger verbal distinction. In a case like this we are prepared to say that scarcity was absolute in its effect—there can be no ascription for what, indeed, was hardly what can properly be called an action at all. One prefers to speak of it as something that "happened to" the two participants, rather than as anything one of them "did."

More interesting, because closer to our typical experience, are the cases where the picture is not extreme —where scarcity is severe, but not as black is to white. In Jan de Hartog's novel *Stella* the hero is involved in a peculiarly delicate situation. He is the skipper of an ocean-going tug whose job is to tow in crippled merchantmen that have been torpedoed. He is deeply involved with a girl who loves him in a sense because of the very fact that, although in one way very much in action, he is nevertheless somehow outside the current violence of the world. As far as his own activities are concerned he saves lives, he is just a tugboat skipper. One night he is being shelled by a submarine which has come so close that he knows her next few shells will sink him. The tug is unarmed. He gives the order to abandon ship, spins the wheel hard over, sending the tug at full speed to ram the submarine, and he jumps. Rammed amidships, the sub goes down with all hands; the tugboat's crew are picked up, except for three men who were trapped below. He has done what he had to do; he has saved his crew—but he is no longer one of the tugboat skippers. He has killed. He finds himself unable to go back to the girl.

De Hartog's story vividly lights up the distinction between the sort of ethical judgment involved in ascribing responsibility, and what we are doing when we simply appraise a state of affairs. Few people could find any blame for the hero, but we know what the man feels when he says that he is no longer a "tugboat skipper." On this feeling no comment is possible, no consolation could escape utter vulgarity.

Then there are cases where some people might indeed want to ascribe blame to some extent, yet where the denouement is so terrible, after the effects of scarcity, that we feel that most of this horror cannot be regarded as subject matter for ascription.

A young girl told such a story to her lover. It was very early in their affair, when they still really knew very little about each other, the time when the first discoveries were being made, when after periods of the new intimacy they had sudden moments of still feeling like strangers. Perhaps he would not have heard her story—certainly not so soon—if he had not happened to notice several outwardly trivial things that nevertheless struck him as important enough to warrant a response from him that inevitably led him rapidly into her heart.

The girl was small and dark and everything about her was very delicately made, all the lines of her body were extraordinarily fine, so that she looked almost impossibly fragile. Nor was vulnerability just a physical appearance with her; it showed in everything she did, in certain small hesitancies in the way she moved and spoke, as well as in the gentleness and grace of her way of speaking, and in her expressions, especially in her eyes which were very large and brown, but secret. There was something almost oriental about her. She was twenty years old, but her body made her look much younger, as did her whole manner, which had a good deal of the child about it—but not a manner assumed flirtatiously or lightly or at all happily.

When he made love to her she behaved quite naturally except that the slight hesitancy in her movements grew more pronounced and once she went through a crisis of feeling that was like the sudden tears of someone whose sorrow has for ages been suppressed. Then he could feel the presence of something carefully hidden, even from a lover.

One evening he noticed something that brought it all out into the open. They had been tired, and had decided not to go out; she had cooked dinner, and they were relaxing afterwards. Under these circumstances he began to notice how much she was drinking. She kept filling their glasses, and it was not just hospitality —she was giving herself much heavier drinks than she was giving him. She was trying to get herself unobtrusively drunk, without his getting drunk too, or noticing what she was up to.

He began to imply that it was getting late, wanting with some uneasiness—some feeling he could not yet define—to stop her drinking. She insisted on having a nightcap. Prompted by a sudden unreasoned instinct, he asked if she had to get herself drunk before she could make love.

He would have claimed that, consciously at least, he

had not been aware of how effective his question was going to prove: years fell away from her face until he found himself looking into the eyes of quite simply a terrified child. Then came the sudden, long-dammed tears and, as she lay clutching him, her shudders were as if the room were filling up with ghoulish forms; shade by shade her story formed all around them.

When she was just sixteen she had fallen wildly in love with a youth not many years her senior. He broke off the affair, afraid perhaps of the intensity of her passion, of being trapped. Her distress was so great that it was over three months before she began to realize that she must be pregnant; ignorance of the need to look after herself had combined with the distracted state of her emotions to prevent her being at all on the lookout for possible trouble. More time passed while she tried to get up courage to go to her ex-lover and tell him what had happened. Her parents, who had always dominated her and made every decision for her, bringing her up to be wholly dependent, she now all at once could not approach or face. For the first time in her life she had to stand on her own feet, and in a situation where she had no notion of how to behave. The boy concerned was totally perplexed; he could not imagine how a girl could be so ignorant as not to have known much sooner or so foolish as to delay even further when she did begin to have suspicions. He even suggested that he was not really the father, saying that it must have been someone later. It must be remembered that his fear was probably nearly as great as hers; also it was true that a long time had passed. In the

[63]

end he simply told her the name of a doctor and suggested that she have an abortion.

As far as can be discovered the girl took this suggestion without much visible emotional reaction or shock; her capacity for such reactions had clearly been exhausted by her interview with her angry and defensive ex-lover. She simply went to see the doctor. This man, however, told her quite plainly that in his opinion it was far too late to do anything and refused to touch her.

There followed a few nightmare weeks of which she could not remember afterwards much of what she did or thought or where she went. She had by then lost all power of intelligent decision and was drifting helplessly toward desperate things. Somehow she got into the hands of another doctor—at least that is what he called himself—and he told her soothingly to stop worrying, that everything would be all right, he would fix things.

She did not know exactly what he was planning to do, but by this point she was beyond critical examination of any proposal, and what was important was that he was assuring her that there was something he *could* do—and would do—and that he would take over, and she could relax and stop worrying and leave everything to him, and it would be all right. What he did was to induce a miscarriage.

"It felt just like having a child," she said. "Once it started I knew all at once what it meant, and I didn't want it: anything rather; but I couldn't stop it then, it was too late, there was no way of stopping it. I had a dead child—you can't call it anything else—I saw it, it was a little boy. . . . Oh God, they cut it up and flushed it down the john. . . ."

When she could control herself she said, "You see I am a murderess. That's why I can't make love."

What will he try to do now, the lover to whom this story has been told? He will try to minimize her guilt, he will attribute as much as possible to the effects of scarcity. His instinct is not unsound—it is a terribly important question. The girl is likely to blame herself much more than anyone—even an impartial outsider —would endorse. But the real horror of the situation only becomes clear to her lover when he sees that no degree of freeing her from guilt will provide any escape from the agony of the appraisals—that unalterably hold—of what has happened. An understanding of the distinction between ascriptions and appraisals is in one sense a "mercy"; the more clearly one sees this the less one is inclined to bestow unmerited blame. But in another sense just this understanding cuts off completely a road of escape; it prevents our confusing any degree of inapplicability of blame with the inapplicability of tragically negative appraisals. In this sense the upshot of the present argument is inescapably pessimistic: being free from blame in no way entails being without cause for regret, in no way insures us against irreparable loss, from inconsolable anguish to the point of despair.

The very effort to offer an escape from guilt, just in proportion to its success, lights up vividly those other horrors from which we can in no way escape, those ghosts which will not be exorcised, those actions which cannot be undone, those scenes which cannot be unlived, those dead who cannot be brought back to life.

About the degree of guilt we can argue and, to an indefinite extent in any given case, excuse—depending on what effects of scarcity we claim to find. It is the appraisals from which we can in no way escape, from which we can in all mercy offer no shred of relief, before whose inexorable truth we are of necessity silent:

> Oh bitter reward
> Of many a tragic tomb!
> And we though astonished are dumb
> Or give but a sigh and a word,
> A passing word.*

* W. B. Yeats, *Collected Plays*, Definitive Edition, p. 295. Copyright © 1934, 1956 by The Macmillan Company; used by permission of Mrs. Yeats. The Macmillan Company, and The Macmillan Company of Canada.

# 3

It is of course the victims of the tragic effects of scarcity who will withdraw, who will become statues of solitude; those who love them might be very ready, at least at the first blush, to try to get past what had happened. Here there is a real asymmetry in attitude —we can to some extent live with and try to overcome what scarcity has done to others; we cannot accept their doing this for us. It is more bearable to hide.

Perhaps the worse victims of scarcity are right (not that they probably are the very worst) ; perhaps it can leave scars of which others—even lovers—cannot for long bear the sight.

Of course it will immediately be said that anyone who has ever loved knows that one does not love someone the less because he is in pain, unfortunate, or prevented by some mishap from achieving the objects of his desire, or from giving one all that in one's longing one would want from him. True, passion often feeds upon adversity, and love grows strong to fight the resistances that chance or the malevolence of others throws in its path. Thus Montague, flying in the face of fortune, eternally seeks out Capulet.

But the worst scars of scarcity leave no slight, no merely romantic, disfigurement; they can strip one to the very bone of everything that may matter to us—everything but the bare fact of blamelessness. What sort of consolation can we derive from the mere realization that no responsibility can be ascribed? One thinker stands out boldly from the history of philosophy for his attempt to offer an heroically hopeful answer to this very question—Immanuel Kant.

This attempt is emphasized with striking force in the famous passage in which Kant compares the moral will with anything that it can possibly achieve and declares its worth to be entirely independent of possible achievements, so that

> even if, by some special disfavour of destiny, or by the niggardly endowment of stepmother nature, this will is entirely lacking in power to carry out its intentions; or if by its utmost effort it still accomplishes nothing, and only good will is left, (not, admittedly, as a mere wish, but as the straining of every means so far as they are in our control), it would still shine like a jewel for its own sake, as something which has its full value in itself." *

The excitement that seems to arise from this passage is no accident; Kant is in fact claiming something which, if it were true, would entitle one to a much greater optimism about life than can ever be derived

* H. J. Paton, ed. and trans., *The Moral Law: Kant's Groundwork of the Metaphysics of Morals* (London: Hutchinson & Co., Ltd., 1948; 3rd ed., 1956), p. 62. Used by permission of Barnes & Noble, Inc.

from notions like the distinction between ascriptions and appraisals. He is claiming something which would release us from untold sorrow—not merely from unmerited guilt.

In the very nature of the distinction between ascriptions and appraisals developed in the last chapter, it is recognized that suffering and failure are no less real merely because in a particular case no blame can be ascribed. The appraisal that something was terrible is just as much an ethical judgment in its own right as is any possible ascription, and does not in any way depend on, or need to be derived from, such an ascription. I was trying to remove unwarranted guilt—I did not claim to be able to put an end to sorrow for what had happened; but Kant is attempting to show that in some sense only the moral will really matters—and that this claim follows from the very nature of ethical judgment.

It must be borne in mind that in speaking of the good will as good, Kant is not referring to anything which this will might possibly attain. He stresses the point that in calling a person's will "good" he is making a quite different kind of remark from what he intends when he describes anything else whatever as being "good." He expresses this by saying that only a person's will can be said to be "good in itself." Clearly anything he says about the good will has to be construed as having the force of what we are calling ascription. But then he claims that the good will is strictly "beyond comparison" with any object which it could attain, thus implying that in some way the subject matter of appraisal does not ultimately concern us—the good will has its whole value in itself!

One could interpret this as merely a rather strong way of insisting that the validity of ascriptions is in no way affected by any possible appraisal; but to look on it thus would surely be to miss the whole spirit of Kant's argument: it is clear from everything he says that he wants judgments about the good will to be regarded as what really matter, not just as logically different from other ethical judgments. He claims that if only the good will were left "it would still shine like a jewel for its own sake." But to examine his exposition in detail is to see that for people to have a good will in Kant's sense it is not enough for them to be blameless; they must also have escaped a number of the subtler instances of scarcity. They are really people of quite considerable attainments. As we shall see, he uses the notion of a good will in such a way that many instances of scarcity are treated as failures to have a good will; the allowances made for the "niggardliness of nature" do not by any means cover all of what we regard as scarcity. Thus it was possible for him to think that what people lost through such niggardliness was not of much moment.

If we are not aware of the full range of scarcity it is easy for us to imagine that no misfortune can affect the things that really matter. Yeats reflects

> Uplift those eyes and throw
> Those glances unafraid:
> She would as bravely show
> Did all the fabric fade;

No withered crone I saw
Before the world was made.*

And that is all very well. But in another mood he admits

I heard an old religious man
But yesternight declare
That he had found a text to prove
That only God, my dear,
Could love you for yourself alone
And not your yellow hair.†

Whatever properties a person has that we could do without, there must be some which we could not give up without giving up most of what he or she means to us. There is no property except blamelessness that the effects of scarcity cannot destroy, and blamelessness is a bodiless thing for a human being to love.

Kant's person of good will, however, turns out on inspection still to have yellow hair—a kindly providence has saved him from some of the subtlest and therefore the worst instances of scarcity. Kant's analysis of the essential nature of morality is based on the situation of this well-to-do elect.

To begin with, what exactly does he mean by a good will? It appears that this is a will which acts "from the motive of duty." It is not quite clear, I think, exactly how this ought to be interpreted. There is a sense of "motive" in which one can lack the ability to call up a particular motive at will. In the sense in which love,

* W. B. Yeats, *Collected Poems,* Definitive Edition, p. 256. Copyright ©
1956 by The Macmillan Company; used by permission of Mrs. Yeats, The
Macmillan Company, and The Macmillan Company of Canada.
† *Ibid.,* p. 240.

affection, jealousy, and the like are motives, we cannot summon up motives at will; but "duty," in Kant's sense, is not a motive in the way in which these are; it is not a feeling or a disposition to have certain feelings. To act, or to try to act, "from the motive of duty" is much more like doing something because we believe we are morally obligated.

> What is essential in the moral worth of action is *that the moral law should directly determine the will*. If the determination of the will takes place in conformity indeed to the moral law, but only by means of a feeling, no matter of what kind, which has to be presupposed in order that the law may be sufficient to determine the will, and therefore not *for the sake of the law*, then the action will possess *legality* but not *morality*.*

The use which Kant makes of "motive" in speaking of acting from the motive of duty may be eccentric, but as long as he adheres consistently to it, he is not departing from his original distinction between a person's good will and anything which he may or may not be able to accomplish.

When we consider the imperatives which determine Kant's good will, an inconsistency appears. A will, whether perfectly good or not, is said to stand under "objective laws." What is the force of "objective" here? We are told at various points about actions being *recognized* to be objectively necessary, and Kant says that a categorical imperative would be one which repre-

---

* T. K. Abbott, trans. Immanuel Kant, *Critique of Practical Reason, and Other Works on the Theory of Ethics* (New York: Longmans, Green & Co., Inc.), p. 195. Kant's italics.

sented an action as objectively necessary in itself. It seems clear that we may recognize certain actions to be objectively necessary, in the sense of binding on us, and do them for this reason, although it may turn out that in fact we were honestly mistaken.

Now if he is to be consistent, Kant would have to say that even if by some special disfavor of destiny we lack information needed in order to form a correct estimate of what actions we ought to do when and to what extent, nevertheless this cannot affect the goodness of our will. He is certainly entitled to say that to act in accordance with the categorical imperative is to do an action which we conceive to be objectively necessary, but in his treatment of imperatives he often seems to want to say that obeying a categorical imperative entails doing an action which an adequately informed observer would judge to be objectively necessary. Obeying categorical imperatives in this sense, however, cannot, on Kant's own showing, be a necessary condition of having a good will, for knowledge of what has been called the objectively right action in a situation is something which we may or may not be able to attain.

Kant, it is true, sometimes says that a perfectly moral being would not act under the constraint of duty, that for such a being there would be no imperative. This seems to amount to saying that if we were morally perfect we would choose an action simply because we believed it to be good, we would not feel self-constrained by a consciousness of duty or obligation. Yet curiously enough, he offers an account of morality almost wholly in terms of notions like duty, obligation, imperatives, and so on, which he has said are relevant only in speaking about those who are imperfectly moral. His justification is usually that he is writing about human conditions, but there is something here which must be looked at closely. It is not clear at first sight just exactly what sort of bearing the varying conditions in which a moral agent can find himself can be said to have upon the goodness of his "willing," or the language in which it is appropriate to describe what would count as perfectly good willing in him. Does Kant want to say that, because of human conditions, human beings are, for some reason, always of imperfectly good will? What exactly can this mean? How has this piece of knowledge been acquired?

We are sometimes told that human beings have to "overcome obstacles"; they have "bad inclinations." The impulses of nature, it is said, hinder man in the fulfillment of his duty. To have a good will, on this view, is to follow the dictates of right reason despite the promptings, and in the face of the obstacles, put up by something called our "sensible nature." The statements in terms of which this view has usually been expressed, both by Kant and by others who have held it, have been partly empirical generalizations about human psychology which it is not to the point to discuss here. Supposing these generalizations to be true, it remains to be seen whether they can possibly have any relevance to statements about good or bad willing, in Kant's sense. If it is the case that our nature contains bad inclinations, then these, together with any other

disabilities from which it has been our destiny to suffer, would certainly impede our will in carrying out
its intentions and limit its attainments in any number
of ways. Even if one's will were perfectly good, such
disabilities would cause what he accomplished to reflect less than perfectly the moral perfection of his
choices, and if they were severe enough might prevent
his being able to accomplish anything. Yet Kant cannot, on this ground, deny perfection to his will. Nor is
it clear how the fact that a moral agent is hindered by
natural causes from carrying out his intentions can
make it appropriate to distinguish between *his* willing
and the willing of some hypothetical agent not so
hindered by using expressions like "subjection to duty"
and "action under a categorical imperative" in giving
an account of the moral choices of that agent.

The notion is still current in some circles that
morality consists in something called the struggle
against temptation. At times, Kant's treatment is simply a refined version of this way of thinking. What are
we talking about when we use such expressions as
"moral struggle," "struggle against temptation," or
"controlling oneself"? If Kant were consistent he
would have had to use words like "struggle" in a
rather special way. He could consistently use an expression like "giving way to inclination" only in order
to speak of a will's being imperfectly good, if speaking
of giving way to inclinations was merely a way of saying that the will was imperfectly good, and not an in-
direct reference to any of the ways in which the will
might be hindered in the attainment of its objects by

any weaknesses in the person's nature. In other words, he could use such a phrase only if it added nothing to what he had already said in speaking of the failure of a will to be good. We ordinarily use expressions like "giving way to inclinations" in speaking about the effects upon our *attainment* of various objects, of weaknesses and propensities of various kinds in our nature which are beyond our control. We would ordinarily describe a person as having given way to temptation even if his failure to achieve some object was due to deficiencies in his character which were beyond the control of his will. But if Kant were consistent, he could never make this sort of use of the expressions in question in his account of imperfections of the will.

In his later work on the "radical evil in human nature," Kant is so determined to show that our nature is inherently "corrupt" that it is hard not to conclude that his earlier stress on the hostility of "inclination" to "rational willing" was at least partly due this bias. Certainly it is in this work that the clash becomes most marked between the two sides of man's nature. Here Kant labors most in his effort to connect our evil willing with something in our "nature." Yet even here he admits that "the source of the bad cannot lie in any object that *determines* the elective will through inclination, or in any natural impulse, but only in a rule that the elective will makes for itself for the use of its freedom, that is, a maxim." * He even goes on to admit that the "primary source" of the adoption by man of

* Abbott, *op. cit.*, p. 328, Kant's italics.

good or bad maxims—the source of moral and immoral choice—is to us "inscrutable." In other words, we cannot predicate immorality of the action of some natural force; to do this would be to turn immorality into a natural phenomenon. After all this, to what precisely can Kant be referring when he says that man is "naturally evil"?

He tells us that, when he says that a man has this innate quality (of being naturally evil) , he means only that it was not acquired in time; that from birth a man has always been so—not that birth had anything to do with it. This, however, does not help, since it is merely a reference to his view that freedom, because it appertains to man as he is "in himself," is outside time, or mere phenomenal sequence. My question can be put again in a slightly adapted form: what precisely can he mean by speaking of a timeless moral choice as naturally evil? Granted that there is some meaning in the notion of a free will choosing evil, what justification can be offered for the assertion that this choice is universal, that for some reason it even must be universal, that not even one person has ever had a perfectly good will? Just because of the hindrances to which we are all subject, one would not want to claim that a will, no matter how good, could ever attain to perfect success in the achievement of any of its objects; but this is quite different from denying that it could ever be perfectly good, for being perfectly good, as these words are used by Kant in reference to the will, does not entail accomplishing anything. We certainly feel that there is something odd about expressions like "perfect virtue," "completely moral," "perfectly good will," and the like because we tend to forget that they are not appraisals of accomplishments—as in the phrase "perfect character," where by "character" we are referring to a whole personality and not just to willing.

Kant's reply to our questions is that man's free choice is "universally evil" because it is "by whatever means, interwoven with humanity, and, as it were, rooted in it; hence we call this a natural propensity to evil." * This seems to me to involve an open contradiction of his own position. It might be the case that there are, interwoven with humanity, various natural propensities which universally impede the achievement of the objects of moral willing, but this tells us only about the niggardliness of nature, and gives us no information about the goodness or otherwise of a man's will, in Kant's sense.

In the next paragraph after that last quoted, Kant writes: "that there must be such corrupt propensity rooted in man need not be formally proved in the face of the multitude of crying examples which experience sets before men's eyes *in the acts* of men." These are "enough to make him turn away his eyes from the conduct of men, lest he fall into another vice, namely, misanthropy." † If Kant had looked more closely at what exactly we do witness when we observe our fellow men, he might have been less confident that his assertions needed no formal proof. What we observe are the various things which people succeed, more or less, in

* *Ibid.*, p. 339.
† *Ibid.*

[78]

accomplishing. We do not observe their willing—indeed, it would probably be more strictly correct to say that it does not make sense to speak of our observing their willing.

I may now state in a more general form my criticism of the way in which Kant uses his noumenon-phenomenon distinction in the analysis of morality. I shall not attempt to conceal my opinion that what is valuable in Kant's ethics not only does not depend on this distinction, but is confused and weakened by its use. If man were what Kant would call a purely "intelligible" being, then whatever else might be true of him, he would, on Kant's view, have a perfectly good will.

> Man (even the worst) does not in any maxim, as it were, rebelliously abandon the moral law (and renounce obedience to it). On the contrary this forces itself upon him irresistibly by virtue of his moral nature, and if no other spring opposed it, he would also adopt it into his ultimate maxim as the adequate determining principle of his elective will, that is, he would be morally good. But by reason of his physical nature, which is likewise blameless, he also depends on sensible springs of action.*

But this is to explain our imperfectly good willing as due to our dependence on "sensible springs of action," which is inconsistent with Kant's own position about the good will. Further, it is inconsistent with his many explicit admissions of the invalidity of such explanations, and his usual recognition that it does not make sense to ask to be told the source of good and bad willing.

* *Ibid.,* p. 343.

[79]

What I have said applies equally to the treatment of the freedom of "rational will" and the determinism of "phenomenal nature" in the *Fundamental Principles*. Kant tells us that, as belonging to the sensible world, man is forced to consider himself determined, but as a rational being, and belonging also to something called the intelligible world, he cannot but think of himself as free. Sometimes he seems to want to say that the life we lead here and now is simply a perfectly determined reflection, spread out in space and time, of a choice made by our rational wills outside time. Whatever this sort of doctrine might mean in detail, it clearly entails taking the view that what he has hitherto described as the failure of the good will to achieve its object owing to the niggardliness of nature is not really to be construed at all as an interference with what the will can accomplish, but as reflecting what in some sense we have really chosen from the beginning. Whatever may be said about this sort of view, it is clearly inconsistent with the other contention which Kant has been making —and to which I have objected—namely, that the imperfect goodness of our wills can be attributed to the operation of something in our sensible nature.

It may be worth remarking that the view which Kant slips into at times, that the will, insofar as it is free, is always perfectly good, has a very long history. It appears to have been held by Socrates, and Professor Paton draws attention to the extent to which Kant seems to have been influenced by the *Phaedo*.* The

* H. J. Paton, *The Categorical Imperative,* Chap. I, p. 6, note; also Chap. II, p. 65, note.

idea turns up again in the philosophy of Thomas
Aquinas. If we were completely free from natural
limitations and hindrances of all sorts, we could not
deliberately choose evil.* It is very hard indeed to
imagine a state of affairs such as these writers envisage,
or to say how we would choose to behave if we found
ourselves in such a condition. There are, however, a
few things which can be said. If these views were correct, it would follow, for instance, that one could not
consistently attach any meaning to speaking of one will
being "better" than another, or, indeed, to any expressions of blame of the Kantian sort which imply that
one's failure to achieve an object was to some extent
due to a failure in his "willing." Kant's views about
the good will (in the passage first quoted) are consistent with its being the case that in fact everyone's
will has always been perfectly good. If this were the
case, however, it would not be consistent with Kant's
view of the good will in that passage to describe this
supposed state of affairs by saying that the weaknesses
of our sensible nature make us naturally evil, using expressions whose usual force implies that a culpable
failing of will can be ascribed to somebody. To say that
all wills are perfect is like saying that all jewels are
equally valuable; connoisseurs could then dispute only

* " 'Nullus intendens ad malum operatur,' dira toujours saint Thomas
avec le pseudo-Denys. Vouloir le mal, ce serait, au vrai, ne pas vouloir."
P. Sertillanges, La Philosophie de S. Thomas d'Aquin, ed. 1940, Vol. II,
p. 187. Again, P. Sertillanges writes, "La liberté du mal n'existe pas dans
l'esprit pur. Si l'homme la possède, c'est qu'il est lié à la matière. . . . ,"
op. cit., Vol. I, p. 228. M. Gilson, also, writes: "Si donc l'homme était un
pur esprit . . . il nous suffirait de voir ce qu'il faut faire pour le faire,
la thèse de Socrate serait vraie. . . ." Le Thomisme, ed. 1947, p. 364.

as to the relative success of the different settings. If it happens that all jewels *are* equally valuable, and hence that talk about them is only a comparison of their settings, it is grossly misleading to go on using expressions which were first employed under the impression that the jewels differed in merit, which were designed to express this sort of point, and which must necessarily therefore suggest to a hearer that a comparison of merit between the jewels, and not merely between their settings, is at issue.

When he began to set out the fundamental principles of the metaphysic of morals, Kant was obviously quite certain that wills differ in merit, and not merely in their attainment of their objects, and he departs from this view only when he imagines himself required to explain and justify odd conceptions like that of the natural evil in human nature. When he is consistent with his original position, he virtually echoes Augustine's statement:

> Seek the cause of this evil will, and you shall find just none. For what can cause the will's evil, the will being sole cause of all evil? The evil will, therefore, causes evil works, but nothing causes the evil will. . . . For the will turning from the superior to the inferior, becomes bad, not because the thing whereunto it turns is bad, but because the turning is bad and perverse. No inferior thing then depraves the will, but the will depraves itself.*

* Augustine, *De Civitate Dei*, Bk. XII, Chap. VI. Augustine's manner of developing his position is of course not free from difficulties, and he falls into confusions reminiscent of those which we have found in Kant.

[82]

Kant's account of moral responsibility runs in terms of technical notions such as that of "obedience to a categorical imperative"; these notions are so construed as to imply that being moral consists in overcoming resistances; and these resistances turn out on examination to be instances of scarcity, so that overcoming them is a matter of being successful in attaining something and not just having a "good will."

# 4

There is a type of argument which has always been used whenever people are forced to admit that there are evils for which no one is to blame. The claim that such bad states of affairs somehow do not ultimately matter can be given a more sophisticated form than we have yet considered.

A thinker taking this line might freely concede all the points about the good will made in the last chapter and fully admit the range and significance of the effects of scarcity and the appraisals that follow from these effects. He need not try, as Kant sometimes does, to pad out the good will by failing to recognize as scarcity important instances of this relation. He could accept the line between ascriptions and appraisals exactly as I have been drawing it. His claim would then be that the whole aspect of existence to which appraisals apply is, in some sense, ultimately unreal or unimportant; that is, he could try to turn the logical distinction between ascribing and appraising into an ontological distinction between two sorts or ways or levels of existing. Many old writers on the problem of evil can be regarded as making an attempt of this kind.

Kant was well aware of this possibility and exploited

it to the full. On the one hand he recognized, as we saw in the last chapter, the truth of the proposition which we express by saying that experience has an economic aspect; he admitted that the good will might be prevented from attaining some or all of its objects as a result of the niggardliness of nature. On the other hand, throughout his writings, there is the recurrent suggestion that the effects of scarcity in some way do not really matter after all. Even in the treatment of the good will there is the implication that the failure of this will to attain its objects through the lack of the required means is not merely to be distinguished logically from a failure for which the will is responsible, but also that it is ultimately of little moment whether the good will is so frustrated or not. The image of the jewel and its setting makes his attitude evident enough. But above all, as we shall see presently, this view of Kant's regarding the ultimate unimportance of appraisals comes out most clearly in what he has to say about the notion of a *summum bonum.*

Kant tries to give his logical distinction between the sense in which the good will can be said to be good and the sense in which anything else can be said to be good an ontological import by combining it with his phenomenon-noumenon distinction: as we are "in ourselves" *qua noumenon,* Kant wants to say that we simply *are* moral wills—scarcity is then supposed to affect only our phenomenal nature. Responsibility belongs to the self qua noumenon, while both accomplishments and the scarcity by which they are affected pertain only to the self qua phenomenon. Whatever the exact logic of Kant's noumenon-phenomenon distinction may be, regarding scarcity and accomplishment as phenomena would imply denying them a certain status. This denial seems to be the point of some of his statements to the effect that the good will alone is "good absolutely," is an "unconditional good"; that other things, and other qualities of the self, derive the whole of what he calls their "goodness" solely from association with a good will; that their absence could not diminish the "worth" of the good will; that nothing can take from its "absolute value," or add to it, for it alone has "dignity" and is strictly above all mere "value." *

There are a number of different ways in which the claim that talk about accomplishment is different from talk about responsibility can be turned into some sort of ontological claim. From our present point of view, however, the objections to any such piece of sleight of hand are much the same; I shall develop my account of these objections with particular reference to the Kantian argument, but it will be obvious that they can be applied to many others. Kant couched his discussions in such an esoteric language that it would be easy to imagine that the views which he arrives at are not such as any ordinary person would ever be tempted to hold. This would be a mistake; ordinary people in discussing ethical problems often throw up the notion that as long as we do our best, not only are we free

* As Professor Paton has pointed out, Kant has a less extreme view of the status of "conditional goods," which comes out especially in his treatment of the "antinomy of the practical reason." I shall discuss this later.

from blame, but what we succeed in attaining in some sense does not really matter. Kant's argument is just the most sophisticated way of putting this sort of claim.

The first point that needs to be made is that, if only ascriptions of responsibility tell us anything about people as they "really" are in some sense, if appraisals tell us only about how they appear to us, then we know much less even than we might have at first sight imagined about people as they "really" are. As we have seen, many statements which people ordinarily regard as ascriptions turn out on examination to be appraisals. We saw in the last chapter that much of what Kant takes to be talk about responsibility does not in fact have the character which it would need for us to grant that it had an ascribing force. If he really wanted to hold that only ascriptions of responsibility apply to people as they are "in themselves," he would have had to be as good as his word, and this would have meant giving us a much more stark notion of morality and being able to say even less than he does about people as they are "in themselves."

I now come to a more serious objection to any theory that accomplishments do not really matter—an objection which applies to many ethical views in which such a claim never appears explicitly. This objection holds even if the argument in question distinguishes satisfactorily between statements about accomplishments and ascriptions of responsibility.

Suppose we try to imagine someone who was not affected by scarcity to any extent, granting for the moment that such a condition is thinkable. Now ascriptions of responsibility would be about his choices (in the economist's sense of "choice"), whereas appraisals of his accomplishments would refer simply to what he was or what his acts were. Just because they are appraisals simply of what someone or something *is*, any attempt to treat statements about accomplishments as being in an ontologically underprivileged class must be based on a mistake. This mistake is implied in the Kantian notion of a world of "moral beings." It does not make sense to speak of a "kingdom of ends" as being made up of "rational wills" just because talk about "wills" is simply talk about the choosing done by people—"wills" are not correctly regarded as a special sort of rather rarefied people. If a thinker uses expressions like "purely intelligible beings," "purely rational beings," it is easy for him to slip unconsciously into a way of thinking which implies that as we are "in ourselves" we are just strange entities called "rational wills," floating about, like the grin of the Cheshire cat, without being attached to anybody. Indeed, Kant sometimes seems to believe that a "completely rational will" would wish to be in this state of happy independence.

This mistake, in its highly technical Kantian form, may seem far removed from people's everyday ethical beliefs and judgments, but the extent to which it underlies much of our ordinary ethical talk may be illustrated by considering certain common uses of the word "character" in phrases like "it's really character that matters." As used in such phrases, it is evident that "character" is meant to be an ascribing word, and the claim is clearly that it is the subject of our ascriptions of responsibility that in some sense "really matters." But this claim only goes unchallenged because the word "character" is so used that what we are talking about when we use it is for the most part simply accomplishments and deeds. If the word "character" were given the much more restricted employment of a genuine ascribing word, we would be much less tempted to identify people with their characters or to think that people's characters are their "true selves" in any sense.

Kant's most usual view, however, is quite free from this confusion. He admits that even people as they are "in themselves" have accomplishments or activities which are distinct from their choices; he simply tries to show that these accomplishments and activities are all in fact perfect, that the imperfect accomplishments and activities which we experience are characteristic only of people as they appear to us. What is being claimed is that scarcity is a mere "appearance." Kant states this view most explicitly in his examination of the notion of a *summum bonum,* which I now propose to consider.

He begins his explanation from an analysis of the difference between statements about morality and statements about the "object" of moral choice; he seems to be holding, at this juncture, that we do not describe a person as "moral" because his activity is directed toward producing certain "objects." * I would agree with this on the ground that a person may, as

* Abbott, *op. cit.,* pp. 244-255.

a result of the effects of scarcity, be trying to produce "objects" which are "objectively wrong," while I do not on that account hold that he is immoral. Ascriptions are not made about the "objects" which a person is trying to produce. "Hence, though the *summum bonum* may be the whole *object* of a pure reason, i.e., a pure will, yet it is not on that account to be regarded as its determining principle." * On the other hand, Kant holds that this *summum bonum is* the whole "object" of "good willing," so that if its conceivability be denied, morality is without an object. He expresses this by means of the somewhat unfortunate statement that "happiness and morality are two *specifically distinct elements of the summum bonum.*" We cannot find by mere analysis of the notion of morality that it involves that of happiness "as if the man that seeks his own happiness should find by mere analysis of his conception that in so acting he is virtuous, or as if the man that follows virtue should in the consciousness of such conduct find that he is already happy *ipso facto.*" †

Thus, in his treatment of the *summum bonum* at any rate, Kant escapes from the first type of confusion which I have distinguished in this chapter, that is, he does not believe in exclusively "moral beings."

He makes a further point which it is particularly important for us to notice. He tells us that

as the promotion of this *summum bonum* . . . is *a priori* a necessary object of our will, and inseparably attached to

* *Ibid.,* p. 244.
† *Ibid.,* pp. 249-250.

the moral law, the impossibility of the former must prove
the falsity of the latter. If then the supreme good is not
possible by practical rules, then the moral law also which
commands us to promote it is directed to vain imaginary
ends, and must consequently be false." *

Professor Paton agrees with Kant in this, admitting
that he believes that the supposition of the possibility
of a *summum bonum* is "a necessary postulate of pure
practical reason, and is inseparable from an uncon-
ditionally binding moral law." †

Exactly the same problem was faced by St. Thomas
Aquinas, who held the same view of its importance.
As is pointed out by a modern commentator, under
human conditions one cannot say that happiness and
morality go together; the truth is that each goes its
own way, the first dependent upon a number of things
which cannot correctly be called moral, despite the
fact that they form the subject matter of morality; the
second dependent only upon having the right intentions, and thus in a sense contentless.‡

With this account of what Kant would have called

* *Ibid.*, p. 251.

† H. J. Paton, *op. cit.*, p. 192.

‡ Thus, in our experience, "la matière et la forme morales ne se re-
joignent point, tout au moins pas assez pour donner satisfaction au
sentiment moral, ni par conséquent une consistance suffisante à la loi
qu'il reflète. Car, ainsi qui l'a dit très profondément l'auteur de la 'Raison
Practique,' 'une volonté libre doit pouvoir s'accorder avec ce à quoi elle
doit se soumettre.' "—Sertillanges, A. D., *La Philosophie de S. Thomas
d'Aquin*, Vol. II, p. 251. "La vertu n'aurait pas de sens, si elle ne cher-
chait à réaliser quelque chose: . . . D' autre part, la vertu devrait douter
d'elle-même, si elle n'avait que par accident le pouvoir de réaliser ce
qu'elle cherche, et ce, par les moyens qui sont les siens propres, c'est-à-
dire par le bon vouloir."—Sertillanges, *op. cit.*, Vol. II, p. 252.

the antinomy of the practical reason in mind, let us consider his attempt to demonstrate the possibility of a *summum bonum*. As a result of his critical view of the limits of the theoretical use of reason, Kant never claims to be able to do more than show that the notion of a *summum bonum* is neither self-contradictory nor excluded by the nature of our experience. In making the latter attempt, however, he limits unduly the extent of the problem facing him by the terms he adopts and his manner of using them. At his worst, he writes as if the problem were confined to showing how "morality" could be "united" with "happiness," regarded hedonistically as "simple pleasure." At other times, he treats "happiness" as equivalent to the complete satisfaction of all our inclinations. Professor Paton notices this inconsistency and also admits that the word "happiness" is unsatisfactory.* Even in its wider sense, the conception of "happiness combined with morality" gives an inadequate idea of what is in fact involved in the notion of a *summum bonum,* namely, that our accomplishment of our ends should be completely unaffected by scarcity. I think that it is fairly easy to show that Kant does not—indeed, cannot—use the word "happiness" in such a way that everything which would count as a lack of accomplishment due to scarcity would count for him as a lack of "happiness." We saw in the last chapter that not all of Kant's statements about "moral goodness" are in fact ascriptions, that some turn out on examination to be appraisals

* Paton, *op. cit.,* p. 86.

[93]

of certain aspects of "our sensible nature"; but clearly he would not have regarded these defects of "our sensible nature" as lack of happiness. Again I hold that many, if not most, of the ethical judgments made by ordinary people are appraisals, but I do not think that it would be at all natural to say that all of these statements were about "happiness."

It is not surprising that Kant's conception of "happiness" should be found wanting just to the extent that the Kantian equivalent of the notion of scarcity was insufficiently subtle. I think it is fair to say that his treatment of what is implied in living under the "heteronomy of sense" fails to do full justice to some of the subtler instances of scarcity. Had Kant been quite clear about the implications of scarcity, he would not have made the mistake, for example, which we noted in the last chapter, of regarding the deficiencies in human nature which are supposed to be due to our sensible inclinations as instances of immorality.

Once we face the full extent of scarcity, the requirements for a *summum bonum* are seen to be much more exacting. We may be able to conceive of some sort of "happiness" being "added" more or less *ab extra* to a person in a life which was in some respects of a different quality from this. It is much more difficult to make any sense of the notion of one's passing into a state where his attainment of all his ends was perfect. For this to happen, everything, every single effect of scarcity upon him, must be thought of as reversed; his whole nature—his very "self" in any ordinary sense of this word—must be melted down and reformed.

Even, however, if we suppose this sort of difficulty overcome—imagining its apparent force to be due, perhaps, only to the weakness of our powers of comprehension and to deficiencies in our language—a quite different sort of problem remains: what precisely is the relation between a person's economically limited accomplishments here and now and his perfection as a member of the "kingdom of ends"? From Kant's many statements on the subject, it seems to be possible to derive two inconsistent answers to this question. The first would be somewhat as follows.

To be completely free from scarcity is implied in the notion of a noumenal self. Granted that we cannot be said to "know" noumena as they are "in themselves," the mere notion of a world of noumenal selves seems to contain the notion that they are members of a kingdom of ends. Qua phenomena, human beings exist under the heteronomy of nature and their morality is powerless to bring about a *summum bonum* in the world of appearances. But, qua noumena, the same beings exist under laws which are independent of every sensible condition, in a system of nature under the autonomy of pure practical reason—which is the fundamental law of a supersensible nature. There are many passages in which Kant seems to take up this position.* Indeed, it agrees quite well with many other aspects of his system. This view reduces the economic aspect of our experience to the merest appearance, and

* E.g., Abbott, *Critique of Practical Reason, op. cit.*, pp. 158, 252-253, and the treatment of 'inclinations,' pp. 256-258, where Kant writes as if there could be purely 'moral' beings, who yet enjoyed some kind of simple bliss.

from this it follows that our limited attainment here and now is equally an illusion—qua noumena we have an attainment which is perfectly "expressive" of our morality, and this perfect attainment cannot be affected by what we attain or fail to attain qua phenomena.

Kant himself was seldom satisfied, however, to leave things like this. His other view, which I think to be fair we must regard as his dominant view, is different in important respects from that just stated. This view comes out noticeably in the stress he lays, at many points in the *Critique of Practical Reason,* upon the need to *demonstrate* the possibility of the *summum bonum.* In such passages he clearly regards this as a special problem and emphatically denies that the possibility of the *summum bonum* can be derived by mere analysis from the conception of morality. At these times Kant appears to be admitting that we cannot derive from the mere notion of an "intelligible being," of a being acting in accordance with the dictates of the pure practical reason, the implication that such a being is unaffected by scarcity.

The "possibility" of a *summum bonum* is then treated as requiring certain "postulates"; the connection between "morality" and the *summum bonum* is not immediate but mediate, through "an intelligent author of nature." On this view the economic aspect of our experience evidently does count; it has to be reckoned with, even at the noumenal level. The effect of scarcity upon our attainment of our ends is not a mere shadow play; the divergence between what we accomplish qua phenomenon and our morality evidently affects us even as we are "in ourselves."

Suppose, however, that we admit for the sake of argument that the notion of a *summum bonum* makes sense, and consider how we can relate our notion of this to what we know about our present experience, both as regards its economic aspect and also the ethical statements which we feel called upon to make about it. If the destiny of a human being is to accomplish fully all the ends of his moral choice, then the effects of scarcity upon what he accomplishes here and now must be mere appearances or, if they are not, these effects must somehow be reversed in another state of life.

In either case, the effects of scarcity upon achievement which we witness can be said to be devoid of significance in the sense that they cannot affect the complete ultimate accomplishment of his ends, which the person concerned is destined to have despite them. If we admit this, we surely render it impossible to make sense of our ethical appraisals; all the appraisals which we normally make involve predicating "goodness," "badness," "improvement," and so on of instances of the kind of imperfect accomplishment which we can observe here and now. We ordinarily assume that we can validly apply terms of ethical appraisal to something which, on the view we are considering, has no more than an apparent significance. Again, all ascriptions that we ordinarily make imply that the person about whom they are made is choosing between alternatives of which we can say that he ought, were

[97]

he completely conversant with the situation and able to choose, to choose one rather than the other. This is not to say that a person's being moral depends on his making "objectively right" choices but merely that the notion of moral choice does imply that there is some alternative which is right.

This is a point which Kant saw very clearly when he insisted that moral choice must have an "object." If the "objects" which a moral agent is striving to realize are mistaken, the agent's morality is none the less, only his accomplishment suffers. But if the reason that the "objects" are not mistaken is simply because there are no right and wrong "objects" between which to choose, it is difficult to see how we can continue to make ascriptions or attach any meaning to ethical questions about how we ought to act.

Thus it seems that the effort to satisfy some of the requirements of our ethical thinking by introducing the notion of a *summum bonum* involves adopting a position about the economic aspect of experience whose consequences make our ethical notions more problematical than ever.

If we identify the notion of morality with the conception of a "will" being "self-constrained" by reason, then it is very hard indeed, as Kant admits, to see how an "intelligible world," which did not contain the necessity of a *summum bonum* being achieved by moral choice, could support such a "categorical imperative." On the other hand, if we refuse to identify lack of accomplishment with immorality, holding a view of the "spontaneity" of human morality, which

Kant would have accepted only in the case of a "holy will," the difficulty may not be so great. We do not now have to explain how a being which would "naturally" follow its "inclinations" can possibly feel "constrained" to be "moral"—indeed, we have seen that it is not even possible to "explain" how a person can ever be immoral, if by "explanation" is meant the assigning of natural causes.

It is reasonable to admit that anyone who is concerned with the achievement of the objects of moral choice can never be perfectly happy or at peace in a state of existence such that he is never certain to what extent the objects of his choice will in fact be accomplished and in which he knows that such accomplishment can in no case be complete. It does not follow, however, that the very notion of moral responsibility can have no meaning for someone thus situated. After all, it is our condition, and yet we have succeeded in reaching a concept of morality.

The notion of morality would only become meaningless if one believed that no moral choice could find any expression whatever in accomplishment, and this is not a conclusion which can be derived from an analysis of the economic aspect of experience, which only enables us to say that the *extent* to which any given moral choice will be so expressed is uncertain.

For the notion of moral responsibility to make sense it is not necessary, as Kant imagined, that we should be able to accomplish all our ends completely; it is enough that we should be able to accomplish anything at all. To say that we are responsible is not to say that we can do anything, only that we can do something.

Kant could not recognize this because he construed being responsible in terms of the notion of a command addressed to a supersensible will. If the command could not be carried out, it was meaningless.

Finally, Kant's ontological distinction has the effect of making appraisals a derived kind of ethical judgment, dependent on ascriptions. If only the good will is "good absolutely," appraisals of accomplishments are made to depend on what can be ascribed. We are led to believe that if no ascriptions could be made— i.e., if no one were morally responsible—no appraisals could be made either. But in fact, just because appraisals are logically different from ascriptions, we can appraise states of affairs even in a situation in which no ascription can be made. Even in a world in which no ascriptions of responsibility could be made, we would still have a type of use for ethical language.

What is true, however, is that the impossibility of solving the antinomy of the practical reason lends special weight in a certain sense to despair. Kierkegaard speaks of the despair of someone who says "I can never forgive myself for it," and points out that if he should in fact be forgiven, then "he might well have the kindness to forgive himself." * No doubt the point is well taken against someone who despairs of *forgiveness;* but we can only correctly be said to be forgiven for things of which we are guilty—forgiving has to do with the subject matter of ascription; we cannot be forgiven for being the victims of scarcity.

* *The Sickness Unto Death,* p. 182.

Kierkegaard's sally, and all like it, thus pass wide of the person who is in despair because of the effects of scarcity upon him, because of things that have happened through no fault of his own, because of his inability to attain the "objects of the practical reason" in Kant's sense. For one in such despair, the only relevant move would be to solve precisely the antinomy of the practical reason, and this we cannot do . . . so all we can do is be silent.

# Conclusion

I have done what I can to sort out the notions of ascription, appraisal, and scarcity. But what are we to think of the failures which are nobody's fault?—of the fact that we may consistently make, of one and the same person, no ascription of blame whatever, while appraising their accomplishments very unfavorably indeed? Suppose that we are trying to decide, in some specially acute case which touches us closely, what to think, knowing the appraisals we would want to make and knowing that we can still ascribe no responsibility or perhaps very little. If we can ascribe little or nothing, in what sense does it matter that the appraisals are what they are?

It seemed to me from the time when I began to think about the matter, that the first thing that needed to be done was to study our talk about "the economic aspect of experience" and then to go into the relation between the things we say about instances of "scarcity" and the different types of ethical statement which we feel prepared to make in different circumstances. In order to do this it was necessary to give as precise an account as possible of "scarcity" and to explain why an analysis of the economic aspect of experience—supposing there is one—should be relevant to the subject of this essay.

Whatever may be the right view about various detailed points which arise over the correct uses of the English word "scarce" and the technical economic concept of "scarcity," we have seen that this concept is related in significant ways to some of the most important notions of ethics. We have also seen that some of these relationships are marked, and some obscured, by the ways in which the relevant words are ordinarily used; also, that greater clarity can sometimes be achieved by deliberately introducing the technical economic concept of scarcity, which can be used in ways in which the word is never, or very seldom, used in ordinary talk. There are a number of parallels to my distinction between ascriptions and appraisals in existing writings from widely varied backgrounds, but on examination they turn out to be significantly different. I have examined elsewhere* some of the concepts used in the past and have offered reasons for holding that in each case these concepts have not had just the set of entailments which they would have needed to do the job at issue. Most traditional ethical writers distinguish in some way or another between something usually called "moral goodness" and what are described as "other good things"; whereas we have seen that what is needed is not less than a distinction of logical type.

* "Ascriptions and Appraisals," *Journal of Philosophy*, LD, No. 24 (November 20, 1958).

The distinction needed is between two uses of language. It is not an ontological distinction, nor a causal one—like that between the will and its effects. Nor is it a descriptive distinction, like that between the voluntary and the involuntary, nor an inside-outside distinction, like that traditionally made between the mental and the physical.

It follows that ascriptions cannot be reduced to appraisals or sets of appraisal statements—and vice versa. I am not claiming—like the supporters of the old ought-is distinction—that there is any word or expression in a language like English which is only used correctly with an ascribing force or as an appraisal. I am simply claiming that when an ascription is made, in whatever form of words, something is said the logical force of which cannot be translated into any set of appraisal statements.

I believe that the analysis of various accounts of "immorality" has shown that the use of the concept of scarcity and the ascribing-appraising distinction makes one less prone to confuse what are in fact references to effects of scarcity with ascriptions of responsibility, than one would be if one relied completely on *ad hoc* judgments. A purely logical distinction thus turns out to have powerful implications for the task of arriving at a humane ethic. I do not deny that people do in practice distinguish quite well between speaking about many instances of scarcity and making ascriptions; on the other hand, there are current a number of ethical notions which would be seen, on a careful analysis in terms of the concept of scarcity, to involve a logically confused account of morality.

An analysis which succeeds in showing a close connection between the concept of scarcity and some of the key concepts of ethics must, to the extent that it is successful in this aim, raise questions as to the status, the importance, of the economic aspect of experience. One soon arrives at some form or other of what Kant called the antinomy of the pure practical reason. Some of our ethical notions seem to make sense only on the assumption, hitherto not recognized as such, that the effects of scarcity in some way "do not matter," or that one can accept some form or other of the notion of a *summum bonum.*

On the other hand, other ethical notions, such as that of the "objects" of moral choice, force upon our attention that economic aspect of our experience whose existence conflicts with the perfection of accomplishment necessary for such a *summum bonum.* Yet philosophers have always felt compelled to claim that what I call the effects of scarcity did not matter. They were not denying the observable fact that many things are scarce. They were claiming that our experience of failing to attain our objects due to the scarcity of the required means does not have the ethical significance which it appears to have, simply because there were other facts about us which we were not in a position to observe here and now but which would have to be taken into account if one were to make a correct appraisal of the total situation. The precise form which this claim takes varies from thinker to thinker, but some form of it is to be found in philosophers as different from one another as Plotinus is from Kant.

Furthermore, some such claim can be implicit in the ethical position adopted by a philosopher who certainly would not defend it explicitly. This is to some extent the case with anyone who simply uses ethical words in such a way that appraising is not recognized as distinct from ascribing. Of course, certain philosophers, such as those of a theistic turn of mind, are naturally attracted by some form of the notion of a *summum bonum,* of a "kingdom of ends," while even they would probably not be prepared to accept the implications about the economic aspect of our experience which are entailed by such a belief.

To sum it all up: What we have been asking all along has been about what is denied and what affirmed, what sorts of gains and losses are at issue, what sort of minding we are thinking of when someone says "His failure does not matter, it was not his fault," "You cannot mind, she couldn't help it," or "You can't blame him, there's no point in distressing yourself." Clearly, I cannot "mind" failures to attain something in the sense in which I can "mind" immorality. Of course, this is only to explain part of what is meant by distinguishing between ascription and appraisal; but it is already something—as long as we are not clear when it is appropriate to blame (ourselves or others) and when only to appraise unfavorably, we are bound to suffer pointlessly. As long as ascription and appraisal are confused, feelings appropriately associated only with the former are bound to get attached to the latter also, and clearer ideas about what sorts of requirements an ascription must meet if it is to be regarded as genuine, and in what manner it is necessarily defeated if certain claims about scarcity can be made, cannot fail to be of some assistance.

Granted that appraisals are not ascriptions and that the whole catalogue of blame words are properly applied only in far fewer cases, in all probability, than we usually realize, what is to be thought of the fact that remains after all the analysis—namely, that we can make desperately unfavorable appraisals?

Only something like neo-platonism would enable us to say "they just do not matter." Even Kant, although he insisted that the good will had its whole value in itself, was unable to maintain consistently that its attainments were a mere setting, of no importance. What sense can it make to say "it is more important to have a good will than to accomplish anything"? Ascriptions and appraisals are not made in the same logical tone of voice; being moral and having a certain set of accomplishments are not two objects between which we can choose. Ascriptions have to do with people's choices, although they are not descriptions of choices, while appraisals have to do with people's accomplishments, although they are not descriptions of accomplishments.

In the sense in which people have various different attainments, their having them concerns us and cannot help doing so. To say of the failure of someone to attain to something specific "That doesn't matter" is essentially to deny that their possessing that particular attainment is part of what we mean by calling them a completely satisfactory person. It can be compared to sketching in the outlines of what we feel such a person would look like. Now if, supposing the picture complete, we were to say, pointing to some attainment which did figure in the picture, "It wouldn't matter if that also were missing," then we are either asking that the picture be redrawn—it was inaccurate before and still contained something non-essential—or we are in effect denying that the absence of any attainment matters, which is to go back to the old heroic claim, or we are at least implying that it makes sense to say that morality "matters more than" accomplishment.

Can we after all give any sense to this last possibility? Certainly in ordinary speech we sometimes appear to be trying to say something very like this. "If I could believe that he had cared, had tried as best he could, I should not mind all his failures or worry about what he became." But is this not to say that we will be prepared to withdraw our ascriptions and substitute appraisals, only if we can be sure we are right? Are we ever denying, when we say this sort of thing, that appraisals could be made, or that they would have a significance of their own? Ordinary speech is full of expressions that are clearly appraisals, and which are nevertheless clearly regarded as, in some sense, important ethical judgments.

We are thus driven back yet again to that consideration which made us abandon the line of escape offered by the concept of a *summum bonum*. To put it in

Kantian language: one cannot remove completely the objects of the practical reason without making morality meaningless, even if admitting this involves admitting that things which will always matter desperately are lost forever, and can in no way be regained. All tragic art is the exploration by the creative sensibility of just this situation.